PATHWAYS TO PARTNERSHIP

Available in the Replant Series

PATHWAYS TO PARTNERSHIP

BOB BICKFORD
& MARK HALLOCK

 ACOMA PRESS

CONTENTS

ACKNOWLEDGEMENTS

Every replant story is filled with names and faces of faithful pastors and church members who made the courageous decisions to do what wasn't easy or common in order for their church to live again. I think of Pastors like Mike Anthony and Slade Johnson who led their congregations to merge with stronger churches for greater gospel impact. In my own experience I think about Adam Tracey, a young man who faithfully shouldered incredible responsibility and dealt with enormous pressures in holding a declining body together and then leading with a steady hand as we began our own replant journey. I think of our founding members, Bonnie Bass and Dottie Brummel who stayed with our church as we replanted, faithfully serving, praying and giving. Rich and Mary Ann Horton and Jerry Henry who have stayed with our church in times of pain and in joy. These faithful partners in replanting have my respect, admiration and love. I count myself privileged to be called their pastor.

I'm grateful for the North American Mission Board its president Kevin Ezell and the Director of Replant, Mark Clifton. These men love the church and are passionate to see struggling churches thrive and live again through the work of Replanting. I'm blessed to work with great teammates like Mark Hallock, Blake Deibel, Brad O'Brien and John Mattingly.

Thanks to my wife Barb for her encouragement and support and for serving along side of me in this adventure we call Replanting. I'm grateful for my kids Alex, Emily and Olivia who sacrificed much as they spent the first years of our Replant journey serving in the trenches. I couldn't serve the work of Replanting without our Elders, Mac McDonald and David McKee and our great staff team, Alex King and Matthew Creath. And I'm blessed to be pastor to a wonderful church, The Groves Church, I love you all!

And I'm thankful for you, the reader of this book as you pray about how God might call you to engage in Replanting Churches for His glory and the good of every community.

Bob Bickford

Let me begin by saying, I echo everything Bob said. In addition... I want to thank my wonderful wife, Jenna, and my children Zoe and Eli. Thank you for your constant encouragement in my life and ministry.

Thanks to ALL those who contributed to this book in some way. In particular, I want to thank Tamsen Sear, Erica Myeni, and Evan Skelton, who sacrificed many hours to help make this book what it is. I am so grateful.

To all of the pastors and denominational leaders who believe God is not done with declining churches: It is a privilege and joy to serve alongside you in this calling to see dying churches replanted for the fame and glory of Christ.

Finally, thank you to my Calvary Family of Churches' brothers and sisters. I praise God for you. Soli Deo Gloria.

Mark Hallock

FORWARD

When I became the pastor of Hilltop Baptist Church in Fort Worth, Texas, the church wouldn't have been featured on any list of the fastest-growing churches in America. And frankly, it wouldn't have been there when I left either.

We were in the middle of a tough neighborhood. Our front door had been busted in so many times that we finally started leaving it unlocked and put a sign on it that said, "Open. Come In!" We didn't have anything worth stealing anyway. The only reason I got the job was that no one else's wife was willing to live in the church's run-down parsonage. The church quickly voted me in 7-0. To this day, that was my only unanimous call—ever.

Language and cultural barriers added to the challenge of reaching our neighborhood. Our community had transitioned to become almost completely Hispanic, and yet we didn't have a single person of Hispanic heritage in the church.

Some churches may be small, but you can compare the church makeup with the neighboring community and tell there is great potential. You wouldn't have said that about Hilltop, though. No one expected much of that little church.

But God did.

Hilltop showed me that you can't count any church out—just because a church is small doesn't mean it can't push back darkness in its community.

I gave the church a choice soon after I arrived. We could either reach out to the surrounding Hispanic community, or we could die. They actually decided to vote on the idea. Fortunately, Hilltop chose life that day. The church chose the gospel.

The church prayed mightily. They told their neighbors about Jesus. They gave sacrificially. By the time I left the church, it had grown to more than 50 people. God used those courageous believers at Hilltop to teach me much about ministry, a lot of which still sticks with me today.

Most importantly, I learned every church matters. Every church, no matter how small, can use what it has to impact the world for Christ. Every church can pray. Every church can share Christ. Every church can give to the work of the Lord around the world. With more than 250 million lost people in North America and billions lost around the world, we can't afford to let any church sit on the sideline of the Great Commission. The stakes are too high. The mission is too important.

If we're going to have any meaningful impact on the lostness of our planet, it will be because churches like Hilltop rediscovered their God-given gospel potential. And it will likely be because other churches partnered with them in the process.

I'm excited about how God has breathed new life into countless dying churches like Hilltop in the past few years. At the North American Mission Board, we're hearing stories every week about churches that were given the same choice Hilltop had: engage your immediate community or die. So many of these churches are choosing life. Eternities have been changed because of those choices.

That's why this book you're about to read is so vitally important. Whether you're at a struggling church looking to re-engage your community or you're at a growing church that wants to help, the time to start is now. I pray you'll take the lessons from this book and put them into practice. Together we can push back darkness throughout North America and around the world.

Kevin Ezell

President of the North American Mission Board, SBC
Alpharetta, Georgia

INTRODUCTION

I thank my God in all my remembrance of you, always in every prayer of mine for you all making my prayer with joy, because of your partnership in the gospel from the first day until now.

- Philippians 1:3-5

My denominational heritage prizes the autonomy of the local church. This facet of our church life works well in that it allows each congregation to determine how it will live out its mission to proclaim the gospel to the community in which it resides. This freedom of self-determination, under the leadership of the Holy Spirit and the guidance of Scripture, has allowed many local churches to flourish across North America and around the world.

Today we know that not every church is flourishing. In fact, between 900-1,200 churches are either in danger of closing or may close in the next one to three years in the Southern Baptist denomination alone. When a local church struggles, it's prized historical autonomy can become a hindrance.

Unfortunately, some of the local churches in our tribe can wrongly view their sister churches as competition. Under pressure and fear, rather than reaching out for help, a struggling church may hunker down and redouble its efforts, only to find that the changes they are seeking to make have been initiated too late to pull the church out of its downward trajectory.

The kind of partnership Paul writes about in the first verses of Philippians is greatly needed among churches today. Programs, events, and renewed passion and energy often can't help struggling churches like other churches can.

We are seeing a new movement take hold, one in which churches reach out to one another; where a strong and healthy church befriends a weaker and struggling church. Together, these congregations are now accomplishing more than they could on their own.

Know this—*partnership isn't easy.* Years of a church going it alone make accepting and adapting to a new partnership a sanctifying work. Because we believe that partnership among churches is not only biblical, but also needed, we've endeavored to write this book. Our prayer is that through this resource, God will raise up pastors and denominational leaders to say *yes* to working together for God's glory and the good of their communities.

In the pages that follow, you'll find biblical evidence for church partnerships; practical instruction on how to partner; the commitments required of partners; and cautions that could hinder partnerships.

May God be glorified; the church strengthened; and men, women, boys and girls hear the life giving message of the gospel of Jesus Christ!

For God's Kingdom and glory,
Bob Bickford & Mark Hallock

PART 1

FOUNDATIONS FOR PARTNERSHIP

Chapter 1

PARTNERSHIP IS VITAL TO A REPLANTING MOVEMENT

We serve a mighty God. A kind, gracious and merciful Lord. And the truth is, our God has not given up on many declining and struggling churches that many of us would have given up on a long time ago. He loves these churches and receives much glory when bringing them back to life and vibrancy. And the amazing thing is that He invites us to be a part of it! The Lord is calling us as His people, as partners in the Gospel, to lock arms and fight, by His Spirit, to stop the trend of dying churches in our communities together.

As exciting as it is to think of even one dying church coming back to life by being replanted and revitalized for the sake of the Gospel, the truth is that in order to reach the masses of people in our world that don't know Christ, *one replant is not enough.* Two are not enough. Ten are not enough. Even a hundred new church replants are not enough! Our vision as the church in

North America must be to see hundreds, and even thousands of churches replanted for the glory of God. What we need is a *replanting movement*. A cyclical movement of churches replanting churches that replant churches.

What exactly do we mean by a replanting *movement*? On the most basic level, movements are about *mobilizing people behind a shared purpose*. Movements happen in our world all the time. Movements happen in the world of business, technology, food, entertainment, or even in the Church. When you look at the spread of the Gospel through the early church in the book of Acts, what you see is a movement...a Gospel movement infused by the Holy Spirit that changed the world, one life, one church and one community at a time.

The time has come for a new kind of movement in the church today. A church replanting movement. A movement where God does what only He can do through His people. A movement where God uses ordinary, faithful pastors, church leaders, and lay people to bring declining and dying churches back to life. A movement that mobilizes God's people behind the shared purpose of replanting dying churches for His glory. A movement where churches with seemingly no hope or pulse come back to life by the Spirit of God in such a way that they not only survive, but *thrive* to the point of replanting other dying congregations. Yes—we need to plant new churches. We need to plant many new churches in order to take the Gospel to areas where people are far from Christ. But at the same time, if we as the Church of Jesus Christ are going to truly push back the darkness and go from a posture of defense to a posture of *offense* in our mission to take the light of Christ into a dark world, we must be as intentional and purposeful in our church *replanting* efforts as we are in our church planting efforts. It is not an either/or, but rather a both/and. Now is the time for a church replanting movement.

Of course, if we are to see this type of replanting movement become a reality, there are several commitments that must be made on the part of churches, pastors and denominational leaders. For the purposes of this book, there are two commitments that are essential to see this movement become a reality.

COMMITMENT 1: OUR LEADERS MUST PRACTICE HUMBLE, RADICAL COOPERATION FOR THE SAKE OF GOSPEL ADVANCEMENT.

Churches are always better together. We are at our best when we humbly and gladly cooperate in ministry together. Just as there is no such thing as a lone ranger Christian, there is no such thing as a lone ranger church (or at least there shouldn't be). We can't do this alone, which is why a replanting movement must be made up of churches, pastors, and denominational leaders who practice humble, radical cooperation. A replanting movement must have Godly leaders at its core who intentionally pursue the joyful sharing of any and all kinds of resources (people, money, programs, etc.) whenever and however we can. In a true replanting movement, this kind of cooperation will not be a burden, but a privilege and delight!

COMMITMENT 2: CHURCHES MUST BE COMMITTED TO ONE ANOTHER AS INTENTIONAL PARTNERS FOR THE LONG HAUL.

Ministry is hard in all kinds of ways and for all sorts of reasons. Because of this, not only must we practice humble, radical cooperation for this replanting movement to become a reality, we must be committed to one another as church partners for the long haul. As Christians and as churches, we are the family of God. Just as when healthy nuclear families are committed to each other, our church partnerships need to function in a similar manner. This means through good times and bad times, mountain tops and valleys of church replanting, we are the family of God. We are a family committed to love, encourage and sharpen one another, journeying together in this challenging yet vital ministry as long as God calls us to it. This type of commitment to one another is essential if we are to see a true replanting movement take place.

Can you imagine what would happen if we began to see large numbers of churches begin to pursue this kind of intentional partnership with churches that are struggling just to keep their doors open? More and more churches are choosing to pursue this kind of intentional, kingdom-minded partnership with congregations in need. As a result, many once-dying churches are now becoming healthy again, engaging their communities and reaching the lost with the power of Christ in new ways. This is the power of partnership!

Children's Sunday School classrooms that had been empty for years are now filled with laughter and singing from little ones each and every Sunday morning. Baptism tanks that had been dry and unused for years are now being filled regularly as lost men and women experience new life in Jesus. Neighborhoods that for years had not even taken notice that a church had been there are now paying attention and being impacted in countless ways through new outreach ministries making a difference in the community. It's happening! The Lord is doing this kind of replanting work all over our country for his glory and the joy of his Church, and we believe *he is just getting started!* Will you and your church be a partner in this replanting movement?

PATHWAY TO PARTNERSHIP

Partnership brings real hope to a congregation.

When my wife, Sarah, and I started serving at Derby Hill, a newly replanted congregation, their story was all too familiar. Derby Hill was once prominent in its neighborhood: the voices of kids echoed in the halls; it was focused on both local and global missions; members were being discipled; and it was a beacon of the Gospel in a community desperately in need of Jesus. Eventually, Derby Hill became an inward-focused, aging congregation, and its once powerful ministry to the community declined with the congregation. They needed a fresh start. They were in need of being replanted.

As members of Derby Hill's sending church, our family was able to serve at Derby Hill during the initial replanting phase. We were blessed to be part of something that was a remarkable reflection and demonstration of the Gospel. A dying church was coming back life! One legacy member remarked, as kids voices echoed in the halls once again, "Boy, it has been too long since we have had any kids here." The focus radically shifted from maintaining the status quo to reaching the community with the power of the Gospel. I have served in several ministries throughout my lifetime, and I have not had a greater privilege than partnering with Derby Hill.

- Jeremiah Heiser, **Member of a Partner Church**

Chapter 2

WHY SHOULD WE PURSUE A REPLANTING PARTNERSHIP?

Why is partnership so important to the health of the Body of Christ? More specifically, why is partnership so important when it comes to helping a replant church experience new health, hope, and vitality? Maybe this story can help paint a picture for why partnership is so critical...

During the summer of 1904 an unlikely partnership was formed at the World's Fair in St. Louis. The summer was unusually hot and people were searching the fair for something to help cool them off. A vendor named Arnold had just what they were looking for... ice cream. People lined up for what seemed like miles to get some of his cool and satisfying ice cream but there was one problem. Arnold was not prepared for the demand and ran out of paper bowls. Next to Arnold's ice cream booth was a man named Ernest, a pastry chef, who was making a Persian wafer desert. Ernest also had a problem, his pastry was not selling. He noticed the problem Arnold was having and took some warm pastry and rolled it into a cone shape. He then went over and showed Arnold how the cone could hold a scoop of the ice cream. On that hot day during the World's Fair in St Louis the wafer ice cream cone was born because a partnership was formed.[1]

This is a beautiful picture of true partnership—people working together in order to produce something far greater than that which they could produce by themselves. Arnold and Ernest had no idea that they would change the way people around the world would forever eat and enjoy ice cream. All because of partnership.

Whenever I think of Arnold and Ernest, I can't help but think to myself, "If partnership could have that kind of world impact for the sake of ice cream, what kind of world impact could churches have partnering together in the power of Christ for the sake of the Gospel?" Just imagine the kind of Gospel-advancing, life-changing, community-transforming impact we could see in our world if churches got serious about coming alongside and partnering with one another. Working together to see God bring dying congregations back to life for His glory through replanting. This is the power of partnership. This is what the Lord calls each of us as individuals and congregations to be part of. Let's consider four key reasons why partnership in replanting is not only needed, but is in fact not optional for those of us who belong to Jesus.

REASON 1: PARTNERSHIP IS BIBLICAL.

Simply put, churches must partner with one another because God has said so in his Word. Partnership is ultimately God's idea! We see this all throughout Scripture. As one writer puts it,

Partnership is an often overlooked, yet vitally important aspect of New Testament Christianity. Although the ministry of Paul and other prominent New Testament leaders was in some ways unique and, therefore, in some ways unrepeatable, the *pattern* of partnership is repeatable. God still provides suitably gifted people to facilitate such partnerships today. Paul used the word "partnership" to describe both church leaders and churches working together:

- As for Titus, he is my partner and fellow worker for your benefit. (2 Cor. 8:23)
- I thank my God in all my remembrance of you…because of your partnership in the gospel. (Phil. 1:3-5)[2]

It is true that throughout history, and specifically in the pages of Scripture, we see that partnership happened between individuals and churches, as well as churches and other churches.

"They helped each other out in terms of *doctrine and practice* (Acts 8:14-25; Gal. 3), they *relocated leaders* to strengthen other situations (Acts 11:19-23, 25-26, 12:25, 16:1-3), they sent *individuals and teams* on short-term strengthening visits (Acts 11:27, 19:21-22; 1 Cor. 4:15-17; Phil. 2:19-29; 2 Tim. 1:18), they sent *money* to help each other and bless the wider society (Acts 11:28-30), and they helped advance the gospel together and *plant churches* (Rom. 15:24; 2 Cor. 10:15-16)."[3]

It ought to be our great desire and joy to follow the lead of Scripture and seek partnership with other congregations in these same ways today.

REASON 2: PARTNERSHIP BRINGS NEEDED ENCOURAGEMENT AND HOPE TO A REPLANT.

When a healthy church partners with a new replant, God brings encouragement to his people. Typically, when you step inside a new replant, you will encounter folks who have been serving for years and are *tired*. Many have probably lost passion and zeal, which is why they have decided to pursue becoming a replant in the first place. It's not that they desire to be dispassionate about the Lord, the church, or the lost. It's just that they've been going so hard for so long that they're simply worn out. It's been a difficult season for that church, and likely the season has been a long one. This replant needs encouragement—lots of loving encouragement that comes uniquely through partnership with other congregations.

God's people in replants also need hope. Many times these churches have lost hope. As a result, they have lost their passion for what the Lord can do in and through their congregation. They need to be loved and encouraged by partner churches in such a way that they begin to believe the truth that God is about to do something great in and through them! They need a new hope. They need the hope to believe that God is just getting started with them. Partnership with other churches can help bring this kind of needed hope to a replant.

REASON 3: PARTNERSHIP FIGHTS TERRITORIALISM BETWEEN CHURCHES.

There's no place for territorialism in the Kingdom of God. I hope you believe this. Sadly, territorialism is all too common. Some pastors and congregations get territorial about their church, feeling threatened by other congregations in their community. What we need are more and more churches that don't get territorial. Churches that purposefully fight territorialism through intentional partnership with other churches, specifically those that are struggling and declining.

The truth is, as churches, we are always better together! Radical cooperation between churches is needed now more than ever. In fact, this type of church-to-church cooperation is a core, convictional value shared by many in the Gen-X and Millennial generations who are now members and leaders of congregations throughout our communities. The value of building *The* Kingdom rather than *my* kingdom (or my church's kingdom) is a huge value in younger generations and in many of the fastest growing, most healthy church planting networks. Much has been written about church plants being far healthier when they work tightly with other churches. The same is true of church replants—they need other churches to help them become what they cannot become on their own. Jesus calls us to work together to make him famous, and it should be a joy to do so! No lone rangers here. As both individuals and churches, we need one another. The mission field is too hard to go at it alone.

REASON 4: PARTNERSHIP RESTORES A GOSPEL WITNESS TO A COMMUNITY IN NEED OF JESUS.

All too often declining churches have become non-factors in their communities. Where perhaps at one time this church was a central hub serving various needs in the community, they have sadly become nothing more than an eyesore to those in the neighborhood. I have visited with non-believers in different cities who would just as soon see dying churches in their neighborhoods disappear and become restaurants or apartment complexes than for them to remain as they are—non-factors in the neighborhood. *This must never be.* The thought of this should break our hearts! How desperately neighborhoods all across our country need these declining churches to be replanted and become lighthouses for Jesus once again. Replanted churches serve as a source of true hope and encouragement, love and healing for people in their communities. The lost and broken in these communities need the church simply because they need Jesus. Church partnership can help restore a Gospel witness to a community.

The bottom line is that we as churches are better together! Millions in our communities need to be reached with the Gospel. Thousands of dying churches need encouragement and assistance from other congregations that partnership provides. This is a good and beautiful thing. Partnership is a God-honoring thing. The question is: Will you and I pursue it?

PATHWAY TO PARTNERSHIP

Partnership helps churches experience the Gospel.

Partnering with a new church replant is such a tangible, experiential way to be reminded of gospel truth. Two ways come to mind as I consider my own experience in partnering with replanted churches: dependency and simplicity.

First, established churches have an all-too-easy tendency to become self-sufficient and self-centered. At my own church, ministries are plentiful. Leaders are abundant. In many ways (although never in every way), the organization hums along. But the danger of comfortability is ever present, and self-sufficiency and self-centeredness are precisely the opposite of the gospel. Visiting a replant is often a much-needed reminder of how my own church used to be: small, dependent, fragile...these are words that describe me! The gospel is brought before my eyes again as I remember the goodness of God in saving people who have nothing to offer. It brings much joy to both the established church and the replanted church to partner in radically God-dependent mission.

Second, replants remind me of the simplicity of the gospel in a culture that often overcomplicates ministry. There is such beauty in the simple singing and preaching of the Word as Christians fellowship together. Established churches like my own, often ministering in a thousand different ways – many of them good, by God's grace – can still benefit greatly from the simple worship of a replanted church. A replant, to be Biblically successful, must keep the "main thing" the main thing, no frills! I intentionally use the term "Biblically successful" because big programs, lots of people, and inch-deep growth aren't the kind of success that a replant (or an established church) should be interested in. They are interested in Biblical success: salvation of the lost and deep discipleship built on the foundation of a simple proclamation of God's truth. And I cherish that reminder in the culture of our day that often majors on the minors.

– *Ben Haley*, **Pastor of a Partner Church**

Chapter 3

BEFORE WE PARTNER:

Considerations for a Partnering Church

Perhaps you are sold on this idea of church partnership and specifically partnering with a replant. You understand the sad reality that many congregations in our country are sick and dying and they need radical help. That declining and dying churches need partnership with healthy churches that can come alongside them and help them be replanted as new congregations. What role can your church play in partnering with these churches? What would it look like for your congregation to partner with a replant in need of new life and growth?

At this point you might be asking yourself questions like, "Can our church do this? What if we don't have a ton of money or people? Isn't this kind of church to church partnership only something large churches can pull off?" Your church, regardless of its size and available resources, can and *should* partner with a replant. And what a joy it is!

A place to start for a partnering church is simply to do some evaluation of its own readiness to partner. Every church is unique and brings unique gifts, resources, and passions to the table of partnership. This is a wonderful thing! What about your church? Can you identify some of the specific ways the Lord may want to use your congregation in a partnership? To help determine this, there are four specific questions every potential partner church should honestly ask and wrestle with as they consider moving forward.

QUESTION 1: DOES OUR CHURCH HAVE THE MARGIN AND MOTIVATION TO PARTNER WITH A REPLANT?

It is one thing to have the desire to partner with a replant, it is another for a church to have the appropriate margin and motivation to actually follow through with it. It is important for the leaders of a potential partner church to count the cost of partnership. What kind of margin does their church currently have? In other words, is their church so busy with programs and other initiatives that it really doesn't have the space to pursue partnership with a replant at this point in time? Is partnership something they should look into more seriously down the road once they have greater margin to get involved in a healthy way? Or perhaps the leaders believe this kind of partnership must become a priority for their church, which means they must look seriously at how to make it happen. We have seen churches that mean well when it comes to partnership with a replant and they want to be involved, but their congregation simply doesn't have the time and space to do it well.

A second consideration for a potential partner church is level of motivation. This means evaluating if the partner church has a burden to help dying churches in need of replanting. Is there a passion for this? Is the congregation motivated to get their hands dirty in partnership? It could be that a church is so consumed with itself that it does not get excited to come alongside and help another congregation. However, it may be that a church would love to partner with and help another, but they are simply in need of more information and leadership that can help mobilize them to act. This is where the leadership of a partner church is so critical. These leaders must cast a compelling vision for partnership and help to create a sense of excitement and anticipation for what God can and will do through intentional relationship with a replant. Most churches are able to create the margin and find the motivation they need for partnership if they are led well.

QUESTION 2: WHAT DO WE HAVE THAT CAN BLESS A REPLANT THROUGH PARTNERSHIP?

There are many churches and leaders that have a desire to get involved in helping with replanted congregations, which is so encouraging. But often they are unsure as to how they can best get involved. This is what is so exciting about partnership! There are so many ways to get involved. Every church has unique resources they can use to bless a replant through partnership, and churches have unique personalities and passions which allows for unique ways to help. The Lord wants to use the uniqueness of each congregation to help build effective Kingdom partnerships. To help a church get started thinking about specific ways God may lead them to partner, consider the following four sub-questions:

Do we have volunteers to share?

There is no greater way to get involved with partnership than to help get individuals and families volunteering in a hands-on manner. Many healthy and growing churches have an overflow of members and attenders who can volunteer time and energy if they are given a compelling vision and purpose for doing so. Sadly, many potential volunteers are underutilized and are, quite frankly, bored. Thy need a new challenge. They need to be stretched. They need a new ministry opportunity where God can use them for the sake of the Kingdom. Partnering with a replant can help provide this very opportunity. What would it look like for a partner church to send a handful of volunteers on a regular basis to help serve the pastor and congregation of this new replant? Can you imagine the joy it would bring for both the volunteers and to the replant? It is vitally important for partner churches to consider if they have volunteers to share.

Do we have money and other resources to give?

Churches should take some time to honestly assess what they can bring to a partnership in regards to resources, financially and otherwise. For some churches giving financially is a primary way to partner with a new replant, while for others it may be that they are unable to give much financially but can bless a replant through other resources. Again, partner churches should consider the unique resources they can bring to the table that will help a replant. Perhaps there are leadership, musical, children's ministry, or outreach and missions resources. Each of these can serve as a huge blessing to a congregation in need.

Do we have encouragement to speak?

One of the things leaders in a replant continually need is love and encouragement. As mentioned earlier, replanting is a difficult ministry. There are unique stresses and challenges involved, and because of this, a partner church can be a great blessing to a replant by simply being intentional about caring for and building up this congregation. Later in the book we will look at some specific ways this can happen, but at this point it is worth considering how powerful it is when a partner church commits to encouraging a replant in this way.

Do we have prayers we can pray?

One sure way each and every church can partner with a replant is through purposeful prayer. Even if a congregation has very little in regard to finances or other types of resources, they have the most important and powerful resource available to them through prayer. In fact, while there are many ways to partner with a replant, there is no greater way a church can come alongside and encourage a replant and its leaders than through seeking the Lord in prayer on their behalf. Every partner church has prayers they can pray. These prayers are deeply needed, and are prayers that God is going to use in the life of this church!

QUESTION 3: THEOLOGICALLY SPEAKING, WHAT TYPE OF REPLANT ARE WE OPEN TO PARTNERING WITH?

This is an important question to consider, not only for the partner church but also for the replant. As we will discuss later, there are different levels and types of partnership your congregation can pursue with a replant. Theological alignment (or a lack thereof) should be a factor in helping you to determine what type of partnership you will pursue. While there are indeed ways churches can effectively partner with replants they are less theologically aligned with, the reality is that where there is shared theological conviction, there will often be deeper and more intimate relationship between the congregations.

Why is this the case? Why is determining theological alignment so important in creating a strong partnership with a replant? Because ultimately, if the goal of this partnership is to help a new replant become a healthy, thriving, God-glorifying congregation in its community, then what is believed about the Bible, Gospel and salvation matters. In fact, it is critical. What is believed about core Christian doctrines will shape how this replant is led and how it functions. If a partner church is not aligned with the replant on these matters, it will determine the amount of money, time, and energy they can invest in this partnership. These theological convictions are not periphery, they are *central*. What a church believes will shape both why and how they do replanting ministry. As a potential partner church, you must discern theological alignment to make sure you can get on board with exactly why, and how, this replant desires to move into the future. Likewise, a replant must also discern theological alignment before they agree to link arms with a partner church like yours.

From experience, we can tell you—it is far better to address these theological issues on the front end of partnership. If these conversations are ignored or avoided, things can get very messy when a doctrinal issue arises unexpectedly, especially if you are pretty far down the road together. Clear and up-front communication in all areas, including theology, is key to effective long-haul partnership.

QUESTION 4: WHO FROM OUR CHURCH WILL LEAD US IN THIS POTENTIAL PARTNERSHIP?

Strong, committed leadership is critical to any healthy church partnership. For this reason, we recommend putting together a *Replant Partner Team* that can help mobilize and lead your congregation in the partnership process. While a pastor should be part of this team, it is important that other individuals from the congregation are actively involved as well. This team should be made up of a diverse group of men and women (and youth) who are all marked by these seven characteristics (add others as you see fit unique to your church culture):

1. A passion for Jesus and the Word.
2. A love for your church.
3. A deep care and compassion for others.
4. A humble heart that desires to serve.
5. A desire to help a replant.
6. A faithful commitment to the partner process.
7. A team player who is easy to work with.

Our encouragement is that the replant partner team tries to meet together every 4-6 weeks over the course of a year, for about 1-2 hours in length. This regularly scheduled time together will allow the team to strategize and determine ways to consistently mobilize the congregation to be involved in the partnership. *It is not the job of this team to carry the entire load of the partnership, but rather to help cast vision and plug in the members of the congregation to use their gifts and get involved in the partnership in some way.*

10 signs your church is (or is not) ready to partner with a replant

In the world of Church Replanting finding and developing partnerships between stronger and weaker or struggling churches is absolutely critical to see a decline in the closure rate of the local congregations that dot the North American landscape. Fortunately, there is an increasing and growing interest in Replanting and stronger churches are looking for opportunities to connect, serve and resource congregations in need. Here are some ways you can know if your church is ready to explore partnering with a Replant.

Ready #1: *Your church has discerned a call from God.*

We often tell potential Replanters; "If you are simply testing the waters and looking for a ministry position, please don't consider replanting." We're serious. Replanting is, in our opinion one of the most difficult ministry assignments anyone could ever take on. Decades of decline are often due to spiritual demise, leadership and organizational dysfunction, disconnection from the community and usually coming with all of those are aging, dilapidated and outdated facilities. In Replanting you're not just starting at zero, you're probably starting at -10. Your church must be called to engage with a Replant. We, in our own strength and wisdom don't' seek out the difficult ministry opportunities--but God calls some to work in the very difficult places.

Ready #2: *Your church understands the pace.*

A church needing to be replanted presents you with multiple needs all at once and each of them could be at threat level red. Forward progress in any one area needing attention and effort can be hampered by needing to move slow, overcoming reservations or fear and providing abundant reassurance to those who are part of the legacy group. Plans and proposals often have to be evaluated and edited in response to "unforeseen circumstances" that threaten to derail or at least delay momentum. Replanting is never 1, 2, 3 it is typically 1, -3, 4, -2, 1.

Ready #3: *Your church is ready to embrace the messiness.*

Replanting a church with existing Legacy members, who are important and matter to God, is a highly relational endeavor. It may be easier to simply think you can dismiss the remaining members but it is not honoring to God to overlook them or see them as obstacles hindering your ministry--they must be seen as your ministry. One of my favorite verses is Proverbs 14:4 says this: *"Where there are no oxen, the manger is clean, but abundant crops come by the strength of the ox."* A mentor of mine summarized this verse through this phrase: *"No mess; no ministry."* If your church wants a partnership with no hassles and no messes then keep walking right past Replanting. But understand this, ministry is always messy.

Ready #4: *Your church embraces a biblical definition of success.*

Most replants don't explode in attendance, baptisms and budget monies given to missions or ministry. Replants typically take 5-7 years to grow into sustainable local congregations. They may never break the 200 barrier. If your church is willing to embrace success in partnering with a Replant as seeing people come to know Jesus, and the community be made noticeably better, your church is probably ready to partner with a Replant.

Ready #5: Your church adopts a servant-not-savior mindset

The church needing to be replanted has likely made decisions that have contributed to where it finds itself today. They know that, you know that. But, there was likely a time when that Church was healthy and vital somewhere in its history. They need help and hope that comes from a servant, willing to walk alongside of them, helping them to become who God has called them to be once again. As a partner church you're not there to be their "savior" you're there to serve them for the sake of the Gospel.

In the same way that Good partnerships are critical to the work of replanting, partnerships that go off the rails create a bad experience for everyone hinder the work of replanting. How do you know if your church is NOT ready to become a partner with a church seeking to Replant? Here are some signs:

Not-Ready #1: *Your church expects the replant to be mini-version of your congregation.*

The local church you lead and serve with is likely a great expression of God's work in a local body of believers. That doesn't mean a church just like yours is needed in another location. The church needing to be replanted likely differs in context--the people right around the church geographically may differ which means that your style of church may not translate as well in that location. Partnering well means allowing the Replant partner to develop the best expression of itself in that location rather than lesser imitation of the stronger church in its location.

Not-Ready #2: *Your church views the replant as a failure before you engaged.*

The church needing to replant isn't a failure. Failure would be doing nothing and not asking for help. But, it's not uncommon for the stronger church to possess an attitude that expresses superiority in some way. Those who asked for partnership and help can spot attitudes like this quickly. It is important to view the church needing to be replanted as a sister congregation who is in need of help and support and good leadership.

Not-Ready #3: *Your church evaluates the Replant by your scoreboard.*

There is a lot of talk, discussion and even debate about what success is for a church. Measuring success by externals is very easy. Attendance, budgets, ministries, and facilities do tell a story but only part of the story. Success for a Replant often looks much different than success for a church or church plant in another context. Defining success as faithfulness to the scriptures, the mission of gospel proclamation, visiting the sick and widows, making disciples, seeing conversions and baptisms, and watching the community become noticeably better are all part of the marks of success for any church including a replant. A Replant will grow at its own pace and have its own expressions of ministries all of which will be unique to who God is making it to be.

Not-Ready #4: *Your church has its hand hovering over the "exit" button.* .

Replanting is a marathon. On average it can take between 5-7 years for a Replant to fully transition, and even then the congregation may not be fully self-sustainable in that the Replanting pastor may have to work bi-vocationally for years or even for the foreseeable future. If a partnering church is looking for a quick in and out then partnering with a Replant will not be a good fit.

Not-Ready #5: *Your church is simply looking for a facility.*

Existing church properties are some of the most significant kingdom resources that exist in North America. Simply put, it is very difficult to replace them in today's dollars, and we never want to see them sold and lost to ministry. Church plants and growing churches are in great need of facilities and property. This need can be met through partnerships and replanting. The need for facility and meeting space can at times lead to perceived pressure on the part of the struggling church and the potential partner church. Strong churches simply looking for space and facilities may overlook the value and significance of the local body of believers who are part of the historic congregation. A church is always more than a building--valuing the legacy members glorifies God and is a good testimony among other churches in the area.

Replanting would not be possible without partnerships between churches. Good partnerships between stronger and weaker congregations will help to accelerate the Replanting movement for the glory of God and the good of the community.

Chapter 4

BEFORE WE PARTNER:
Considerations for a Replant

A few years ago, I was meeting with a new church planter for coffee. After he shared with me the exciting vision of this new congregation and its desire to make sold-out disciples of Jesus in a largely unchurched neighborhood of Denver, I looked at him and said, "I'm in! How can I help? What are some ways our church can partner with you and this church plant?" At that moment, there was an awkward silence. He then looked at me with sort of a confused look on his face. "Uh, if I'm honest, I really haven't thought much about that. Prayer and money is always nice."

Oh boy. "Prayer and money is always nice?" Well, that is a true statement. I've got to give him that. But…really? I'm sitting here as a potential partner with your new church plant and that's all you've got? To tell you the truth, I felt embarrassed for this young church planter. This sweet guy had a great vision for his church, but he had not thought through some of the most basic components for building effective partnerships with other churches that would be absolutely critical for the long-term health and growth of this new congregation. While I tried to lovingly offer a few words of counsel and coaching to him on how to build partners, we did not move forward in formal partnership with this church plant at that point in time.

I share this story to illustrate the importance of having an intentional strategy for church partnership. Unlike my church planting friend, the leaders of a new replant must have a thoughtful game plan for getting other congregations on board and connected to the ministry of their church. Before partnership can begin to develop, it is critical for leaders in a replant to thoughtfully and prayerfully ask and answer two key questions.

QUESTION 1: WHAT ARE SOME OF OUR PRIMARY PARTNERSHIP NEEDS?

The first question a replant should ask pertains to the various needs they have. While there are probably all kinds of needs present in this congregation, they typically fall together in groups. The leaders of the replant should take some time together and list some of the present needs under the following categories.

Need 1: Relationships

These relate specifically to the ongoing care and encouragement that can come from a partner church. How can a partner church help to encourage the replanter, the replanter's family, and the leaders and members of this new replant? What would some of these relational needs be?

Need 2: Finances

Typically, new replants need financial help and assistance of some kind. A replant should be clear on what exactly these needs are, and which needs a partner church might be able to help with.

Need 3: Leadership

Replants are often short on strong leaders. What are currently some of the specific leadership needs in the replant? Music? Children and youth? Other?

Need 4: Volunteers

Every replant needs volunteers. However, the leaders of a replant should think through carefully where they currently need volunteers the most. How might volunteers from a partner church be best utilized? A game plan is needed for this, as volunteers from partner churches will become frustrated without a clear vision and plan.

Need 5: Equipment and Supplies

What are some of the main equipment and supply needs in the replant? For example, is a new sound system needed? New signage? A new coffee bar? What about fresh paint in the classrooms? Are new children's toys needed in the nursery? Perhaps new Sunday School curriculum? What about copies for the church bulletin and other teaching resources?

Need 6: Prayer

Putting together a list of specific prayer requests can be extremely helpful in mobilizing church partners to pray for the replant. Update these prayer requests regularly and make them easily available for partner churches to use on an ongoing basis.

QUESTION 2: HOW WILL WE NURTURE OUR RELATIONSHIP WITH A PARTNER CHURCH?

Like any relationship, partnership takes intentionality. To build a close friendship between churches takes work and time. What are some of the particular ways a replant can nurture its relationship with a partner church? Here are five very practical relationship building strategies for a replant to implement.

Strategy 1: Communicate Consistently

The leaders of a replant should work hard to over-communicate with church partners. Communication should be clear and consistent. There is nothing worse than for a partner church to be out of the loop with what is happening with a replant they are trying to help. On the other hand, there are few things that stoke the passion for the partner relationship than keeping partner churches in the loop with what all is happening in the replant.

Strategy 2: Celebrate Victories

Invite partner churches to celebrate victories in the replant! For example, when there is a baptism or baby dedication, that is a victory to be celebrated. A replant should invite partner churches to celebrate these with them. A replant should work to share the wonderful ways God is working to change lives through this new work with partners.

Strategy 3: Share Struggles

While celebrating victories with partner churches is appropriate, so is sharing struggles. Replanting is hard—it just is. A good partner church understands this, which is why they will want to be aware of the specific challenges the replant is experiencing. Churches are called to share in one another's sufferings that we might pray for and serve one another. Being open and transparent with some of these struggles is critical if this is to happen.

Strategy 4: Practice Thankfulness

Have you ever given a gift to someone who did not offer thanks of any kind back to you? My guess is you have. Of course, we don't give gifts in order to be thanked, but a thank you sure is appreciated. In fact, doesn't it make you even more eager to give to this person again in the future? The same is true in partnership. A replant should seek to practice consistent, purposeful gratitude and thankfulness with its partner churches. Expressing sincere thankfulness will bring encouragement to the partner church and will help strengthen the relationship between the two churches even more.

Strategy 5: Pray for the Partner Church

They are few things that nurture any type of relationship more than prayer. Whether it is a relationship with a spouse, a child, or a friend, God uses prayer to grow deeper intimacy and connection. In the same way, prayer is vital to nurturing a replant's relationship with a partner church. As a result, a replant should be very purposeful in prayer. Ask the partner church to share specific prayer requests for their church and those in the congregation. The replant should commit to praying for these things and regularly let the partner church know they are being prayed for. Watch how God uses prayer to grow this important relationship for his purposes.

how can a replant find church partnerships?

Having pastored established churches since 2001, I made some unfortunate assumptions as God moved us into this season of leading a replant. Because I had experienced a certain rate of growth in each of the previous churches I served, it made perfect sense to me that the same would happen in a replant.

Leading a replant, however, is very different from pastoring an established church. Leading a replant church requires church partnerships. A replant church is resource hungry, people are needed, financial resources are needed, and you can't do it alone. I am continuing to learn how to find, maintain, and cultivate new partnerships.

Here are a few ways we have thus far entered some strong, partnering relationships.

ministry friends

You likely have friends in ministry – pastors, youth pastors, missions committee members, deacons, or simply friends who are members of other churches. Contact them, reconnect – share your call to replanting. Create a prospectus that provides a clear and captivating picture of the way things look now (the negative present) contrasted by how they will look moving forward (the positive future). Ask these friends to become prayer partners and encourage them to share your replant opportunity with their friends, Sunday school classes, and church staff. Your relationship with members of other churches becomes a vital resource in the first phase of seeking out church partners.

missions conferences

Our replant is taking place in a different state from where we previously lived. The state we left in order to replant became a huge source of church partnerships – more than I could have imagined! Through sharing our vision with all our ministry friends, opportunities opened up beyond our personal reach. I was invited to that state's missions conference to share about our replant. This allowed us to connect with many more churches looking to partner with church plants. I would encourage you to look for any opportunity to be part of a missions conference (whether at the national, state, associational, or local church level) where you can share your captivating vision and connect with other mission-minded church leaders.

local association/director of missions

In a matter of weeks, there will be a Replanting Certification Seminar at the NAMB headquarters in Alpharetta. There are more than 250 directors of missions signed up to take part in this very first-of-its-kind seminar. It excites me, because our replant situation would not have happened without the leadership of our association and director of missions. That so many DOM's are beginning to get excited about the potential for replanting is huge! And it's huge in terms of finding church partnerships. If the leadership of your association supports the work of replanting, there is already associational buy-in. That means you already have a network of churches familiar with your replanting. Even if you are new to the area (as I was), your replant situation is a known need. For us, this meant opportunities to speak to area churches about our need and our story. This opportunity opened doors to other associations (even in other states) that have invited us to share with their associational church leaders about our replant. Great DOMs and associational leaders are a huge resource for church partnerships!

churches looking for partners

This point is more of a sub-point of all the above, but very pertinent. While not all churches are looking for "hands-on" opportunities to partner in church planting or replanting, many are looking for such opportunities. Many are not yet aware of "replanting." In many ways, the struggles of a replant are much more relatable to established churches than are those of the "from scratch" church plant. The demographics of attendees (at least at the beginning) are much the same. The need for new vision and re-energized evangelism efforts are shared. In a replant, the new focus, direction, and vision will resonate well with established churches. We have been connected to partners by our state convention and association (and ministry friends) who had been contacted by churches seeking to partner with planters and replanters. There are ready-made partnerships out there!

some practical encouragement

1. **Be clear and direct.** Don't beat around the bush, but share your specific needs to potential partners with clarity. Many larger churches are ready to send teams to do "their thing," even though it might not be what you need (or even fit your vision).

2. **Be flexible.** Sometimes church partners cannot meet your need with specificity, but still want to help. We have found there are times we require partners to fit the vision and other times we adapted to fit our partner's gifting and ability – to the glory of God and expansion of our own vision.

3. **Be responsive.** Communicate often and clearly. When they email or leave a message, get back to them. Don't leave people hanging. While I have failed at this more than I'd like to admit, we also have entered partnership with several churches that had tried to partner with other local planters but never received prompt returned communication.

4. **Be prepared.** We launched strong because we had many partners on the front end, helping in numerous ways. But you will need partners as much (if not more) in Year 2 (and I hear even in Year 3). In a replant, be ready to see decline before you enter a true season of growth. All who are present at the launch – whether it's the previous church's remnant (and tithers) or curious community folks – most likely not be there in Year 2. Plan to forge some lasting church partners who will be ready to strengthen their support as the replant takes root.

Jason Helmbacher
Replant Pastor, Church at Affton
St. Louis, MO

PART ONE
DISCUSSION QUESTIONS

Foundations for Partnership

1. We are living in a day when church revitalization and replanting is needed more than ever before. Discuss some of the reasons why partnership is vital to a replanting movement in North America and around the world.

2. Why should a partner church seriously consider pursuing a replanting partnership? What are some of the blessings and benefits that come from an intentional partnership for a replant? For a partner church?

3. What are some of the real challenges churches (both a replant and a partner congregation) must consider before pursuing a partnership?

4. Discuss some of the key considerations for a partnering church that are laid out in chapter 3. Why are these considerations so important before jumping into a partnership?

5. Discuss some of the key considerations for a Replant that are laid out in chapter 4. Why are these considerations so important before jumping into a partnership?

6. What are some of the things that excite you most about the potential for partnership? Why?

PART 2

DEFINING THE PARTNER
RELATIONSHIP

·

Chapter 5

WHY DEFINING THE RELATIONSHIP MATTERS

As the father of two daughters, I've developed a keen sense for picking up the potential blossoming of a dating relationship. The signs are fairly tell-tale; frequent appearances made by a particular boy who "happens" to be at the game, concert or other event my daughter is attending, the mention of a new name by my daughter and the inclusion of a new friend in the group that is "just going to hang out" all point to the likelihood of this becoming a "thing."

As the incidences grow more frequent at some point I will make a careful, low-key inquiry and ask; "So, tell me about *(boy's name)*." At that point the conversation which follows will be an enlightening one, I'll be told that the person is "just a friend" or "someone that likes me" or "someone I'm hanging out with but not dating" or "my boyfriend."

There are a host of terms that describe the types of potential relationships which seem to change every other month and confuse me beyond belief—but that's the nature of dating and being a dad these days. What I believe is an official dating relationship and what stage my daughter is at with this new guy don't always coincide, which leaves me needing more definition to understand what's really happening.

In the world of church partnerships, it is important to define the relationship. Failing to do so can lead to misunderstandings, confusion, conflict and hurt that impact the kingdom work of replanting churches for the gospel and God's glory.

CLARITY - THE FOUNDATION OF PARTNERSHIP

When two churches consider partnering for the sake of the gospel, it is imperative to take the time to labor over getting everything out on the table in terms of what it could, will and does mean for this partnership to be official.

This doesn't happen in one or two conversations—it happens over an extended period of time in multiple settings with multiple leaders, with written records of meeting notes, with questions noted and answered in later gatherings.

One of the first and most foundational questions to answer as you consider your partnership is this: *Why do we believe God is leading us to consider partnering together for the Gospel?*

Often the two churches considering partnering together give less time to answering this question and more time to the questions of logistical and stylistic leadership issues that will come with partnership. While those are important matters, they can each be derailed when the two churches lack clarity on why they are coming together, joining resources and people, taking the lead or agreeing to being led.

When you have the answer to *why* you believe God is leading you toward partnership, you must compose that answer into a statement and share it with your people. Read it prior to your members meetings where you will discuss the potential partnership, put it at the top of your proposal documents, read it at your leadership team gatherings. This statement represents the vision that God has birthed in your two churches for greater gospel impact in your context.

This statement can help you resolve "lesser" matters that can derail partnerships when the big picture is lost as you move toward formalizing the partnership and necessary and required adjustments.

Sample Partnership Purpose Statement

We believe that [Partner Church] and [Replant Church] are called by God to partner together to reach [geographical location] for Christ. We believe that our combined resources will enable us to do more together than we could do apart.

RESPONSIBILITY - HOW WE BOTH WILL CONTRIBUTE TO THE MISSION

Partnerships form in part because of an honest evaluation on the part of those considering becoming partners. One may feel compelled to serve the kingdom by utilizing their resources and experience to further the Gospel and kingdom impact in a particular area. Another realizes that their church finds itself in a place of need and believes that significant ministry can still go forward but that will require assistance from the outside.

True partnership is realized when both churches understand clearly what they bring to each other. A clear understanding of their strengths, resources and expertise combined with the Godly humility to admit where they are weak and struggle sets the stage for strong partnership.

It is imperative that each potential partner understands clearly what their strengths and weaknesses are as they explore coming together. We recommend that each church do a self-analysis and compose a strengths and weakness chart on their own, and work toward shaping the results as they progress in their partnership discussions.

After sharing the findings from the strengths and weaknesses assessment, it will be important to determine who leads in the major areas of the church: Preaching, administration, evangelism/outreach, worship, children/youth, etc. Add this responsibility and rolls sheet to your growing list of partnership documents for the sake of clarity and understanding.

Certain partnerships may form where one church is on the lower end of the health and vitality scale. *It is important to understand that even a weaker church has something valuable to contribute to the partnership.* An older congregation often has a faithful group of praying and serving saints who can find vital places of service in the forming partnership between the two churches. We encourage you to labor hard in finding ways they can make a meaningful contribution moving forward.

ACCOUNTABILITY - WHO WE WILL ANSWER TO

Everyone makes decisions according to a process they understand and feel comfortable with. Every church has a process that guides them in their decision making—one they have grown accustomed to or comfortable with.

When two churches join in partnership, the issue of accountability has to be worked out with patience, prayer and grace. It is not uncommon to encounter fear or misunderstanding about the decision-making process, leadership structure, terms and guidelines. One church may vote on many things, where another only affirms the major items/issues impacting the congregation.

Working out the decision-making structure and accountability lines help both potential partners understand how decisions will be made, who will lead and how those in leadership will be accountable. The greater the differences in the way partner churches are led require greater investments of time, conversations and teaching to leaders and church members.

PATHWAY TO PARTNERSHIP

Partnership is a display of the kingdom of God.

From the beginning of creation, God has been about having His people spread His glory to the ends of the earth. The Apostle Paul tells us in the book of Ephesians that the church is the focal point of his glory. There is something sweet and amazing about being part of what God is doing through the local church.

Recently, my family and I were sent out from our church to help replant a declining congregation. I would strongly encourage churches to partner with church replants, and here's why.

First, partnering with a replant shows that you are more concerned with God's kingdom than you are with building a kingdom for yourself. As churches, it's tempting to want to hold on tightly to our best people. It's tempting to want to use our budgets, and time, and resources to pour into our own local church. It might feel like we're shooting ourselves in the foot to send our resources outside of our own body. But, when we make a decided effort to pour into church replants it is a very tangible way to show that we are about God's kingdom and not our own kingdom. Jesus loved the church to the extent of giving his life for her. Would Christ's love for his bride motivate us to sacrificially give for her as well!

Second, partnering with replants will bring spiritual life, excitement, and fruit to your own congregation. It's counter intuitive from the world's standpoint, but when we aren't insular, when we are externally focused, God actually works within us to grow us. When churches partner with replants, not only is life and strength brought to the replant, but to the partnering churches as well.

Lastly, I would encourage churches to partner with replants as a way to show that we aren't in this alone. One of Satan's greatest weapons in our personal lives, and in the lives of our church is isolation. Larger churches which are isolated tend to become stagnant and stale. Replants that are isolated tend to whither and pastors can wallow in loneliness. But, when the two link arms and the body of Christ comes together, we're able to combat the pitfalls and dangers of isolation as those who are united with one Spirit and one mission.

Again, I would encourage churches to partner with replants. Initiate! Look for opportunities in your area. Seek out those new pastors and churches and see how you might link arms with them. Do that and see what the Lord does in and through your church!

– *Adam Grusy,* **Member of a new Replant**

Chapter 6

TYPES OF PARTNERSHIPS

In the world of replanting, a common mistake is to believe that there is a one-size-fits-all approach to partnership. This developed from some of the early innovating churches who had one type of partnership they repeated over and over with great success.

As we have worked with different churches, we've discovered many types of partnerships and are thankful that there is not only one-size or type. We believe there are *many* different ways churches can form partnerships, and we believe that each of them has their place and are needed. Some models of partnership do cost more for those involved, whether it be the stronger church or the weaker church.

The cost isn't always in terms of resource; often it is associated with identity or tradition. A new partnership may change the nature and look of a church—but we can and should expect that the mission and the message remain the same—

proclaiming the Gospel and serving the community for the glory of God.

TYPES OF PARTNERSHIP EXPLAINED

Type 1: Equipping

The intentional development of ministry capacity and skills from a stronger church to a weaker or struggling church through shared or site-specific training by skilled ministry leaders and members.

Commitment Level: **Low**
Commitment Type: **Instructional**
Commitment Financial Cost: **Low**

An equipping partnership provides the opportunity for a strong church to serve a struggling church through focused training in any particular ministry area with the goal of empowering them with the knowledge, skills and process or plan to move forward in a ministry area. This could take the form of allowing leaders to attending equipping events at the partner church or through sending teams to do training for the receiving church.

Type 2: Coaching

A personal, intentional partnership between the leaders of strong church and the leaders of struggling church where ministry staff/leaders/volunteers receive specific ministry role related coaching.

Commitment Level: **Medium/High**

Commitment Type: **Relational**

Commitment Financial Cost: **Low**

In recent decades there has been an explosion in the world of professional coaching. A professional coach is one who comes along side and provides feedback and insight for an individual on performance related matters for the specific area they have been asked to "coach." A qualified ministry coach is one who has experience and expertise in a particular area of ministry leadership and can provide skills-based instruction for a pastor, worship leader, youth leader, administrator, etc.

A coaching partnership may be informal or formal, it should be focused on a specific ministry area with clear assignments and activities and for a specified time frame. This type of partnership is mostly personal in nature and the members of the churches may or may not be aware that such a partnership exists.

Type 3: Resourcing

The commitment of finances, personnel and/or materials to serve the struggling church in its accomplishment of its ministry objectives and goals.

Commitment Level: **Medium/High**
Commitment Type: **Organizational**
Commitment Financial Cost: **Medium/High**

There is certainly biblical precedent in the sharing of resources from congregation to congregation for the accomplishment of ministry and to provide relief (2 Corinthians 8). Stronger churches often have an abundance of resources in finances, material possessions and personnel. A struggling church likely does not. One of the key aspects in a resourcing partnership is the development of a *true* partnership. In some cases a struggling church who is seeking a stronger partner may simply want the resources without the relationship. In some cases where there is simply an exchange of material possessions (chairs, audio/visual equipment etc.), there may be little need of a long term or involved relationship.

However, when the resources involve finances and people, it should be expected that there will be some level of accountability and responsibility for those resources as they are granted.

What we mean to say is this: a struggling should not expect to receive money and people without assuming accountability or responsibility to the resourcing church. We too often encounter a weaker or struggling church who believes that more money and more people will be the solution to their needs. We've not found this to be the case. In fact, if you de-layer the last few years/decades, typically what you will find is that the struggling church had people and money at one point, and over time made decisions or mishandled crisis that lead to their decline. Often it is a decline that will not be reversed without clear self-evaluation and repentance.

It is totally appropriate for those making resources commitments with money and people to expect a level of accountability and responsibility from the receiving church.

Type 4: Merger

The partnership of a stronger church and a weaker/struggling church where the stronger church takes the lead as the two become one congregation taking on the identity and accepting the leadership of the stronger church.

Commitment Level: **High**

Commitment Type: **Total**

Commitment Financial Cost: **High**

The word *merger* is a business term that often carries with it the connotation of takeover by a stronger and the absorption of a lesser. As is true in the business world, mergers often leave those who were "merged" feeling as outsiders. In the world of church replanting, this doesn't have to be so, but we recognize it is a frequent feeling and perspective. That being the case, the stronger church and its leaders would do well to honor the church and its history as much as possible.

Type 5: Marriage

The intentional joining together of two congregations for the purpose of greater gospel impact.

Commitment Level: **High**

Commitment Type: **Total**

Commitment Financial Cost: **High**

In this partnership, two distinct churches come together to become one new church. This could be any combination of a stronger church or struggling church, two church plants, or an established church and a new church plant.

Both realize that their individual identities will cease and they will become one new church. Like in a marriage, one may assume the name of the other, or they may combine their name in some way if they do not choose a completely new name.

There are many legal considerations to be worked through as one or both entities will need to be dissolved and one be prepared to receive the assets and obligations of the other or both will become part of a completely new church. We highly recommend you consult your local church law professional regarding the specifics of how to complete a marriage.

In some cases, it is easier for one church to remain and the other to dissolve so both may operate under a DBA (Doing Business As) designation from the state in which they reside.

Type 6: Adoption/Campus

The enfolding of a struggling/weaker congregation into a stronger church which typically has resident members who travel from the immediate area in which the adoptee church is situated.

Commitment Level: **High**
Commitment Type: **Total**
Commitment Financial Cost: **High**

Churches that have a geographical reach spanning several miles or cities are well suited to this type of partnership. A weaker or struggling church may find itself within the geographical reach zone of a regional church which draws people from the area in which it resides. In these cases, an adoption/campus partnership is worth considering. This partnership allows for people to worship in their community and actually increases their impact, as many unchurched or de-churched residents would prefer not to drive to another community to attend worship and engage in the life of a local church.

The congregation being adopted is brought into the family and shares the name, identity, ministries and all programming of the church by whom they are being adopted. Depending upon the governance style, the adopted church may have local leaders or be led by leaders who are part of the larger overall central church. This varies and may transition over time depending upon the structure of the church assuming responsibility for the local congregation.

Costs associated with building remodel and upgrades may be high, as often the adopted church has not maintained its physical property in the same way as the adopting church has.

Like the merger, it is important to celebrate and value the members and leaders of the church which is being adopted.

Type 7: Network/Family

A struggling or weaker church becomes part of a network or family of churches with a recognized ministry approach, philosophy and style and demonstrated effectiveness.

Commitment Level: **High**

Commitment Type: **Total**

Commitment Financial Cost: **High**

Although it has similarities with the adoption and campus models of partnership, the network/family model does have some differences. It is likely true that the church joining the network or family is a greater distance away from the parent church. It can be in a different city, county or even state.

A network or family church often has leaders who have been trained and equipped to be sent out to lead the local congregation coming into the family or network.

The bonds or relational connections with the network and family are kept strong and the local leaders are led by a local pastor who is accountable to the network leadership while local leaders are being raised up and installed into leadership.

Type 8: Replant[4]

The process in which members of a church facing imminent closure discern God's leadership to dissolve their current ministry and work with other churches or denominational bodies to begin a new church for a new season of ministry in their community.

Commitment Level: **High**
Commitment Type: **Total**
Commitment Financial Cost: **High**

This model of partnership carries with it both the greatest risk and opportunity for reward. In a replant, the members determine to dissolve the church as it has been, not knowing what will be like in the future. The decision to replant may come before partners have been identified or recruited. A replant may not yet have a pastor called to lead them as they move forward.

Every replant requires partners, and every replant is hungry for resources. The investment by the local association, state convention or national denomination is key in that they serve the local congregation by guiding, encouraging and providing counsel as next steps are taken.

A replant starts over or begins again with new leaders, a new decision making process and a new qualified and called pastor who will lead them forward. This means that members have agreed to put everything on the table and hold all things loosely so that their church may be truly replanted for God's glory.

Replanting this way is a high-risk endeavor, but it is one which can bring about the renewal of a vital Gospel outpost in the community.

BEING HUMBLE AND SERVANT-HEARTED

Good leaders have the gifting and ability to see things as they are, and possess the clear vision of how things could and should be. Great leaders are those who know how to lead the people from where they are to where God wants them to be. Great leaders know that even in the face of fear and uncertainty, God can always be trusted to do what is right and good.

A recurring theme in Jesus' teaching on leadership involved some things that seem to be lacking in some leaders' lives today: humility and servant-heartedness.

Guiding struggling churches to consider their future is one of the most challenging aspects of the ministry assignment that God has granted us. There are times when our vision is clear and our hearts are emboldened to speak the truth plainly, and there are moments when that is tempered by the whisper of the Holy Spirit.

As you lead churches to consider pathways to partnering together, you'll need boldness and gentleness, and you'll need to adopt the posture of a humble servant.

In our fast paced and impatient culture, we may not value long conversations and personal visits to provide assurance and answer questions for the umpteenth time. We may find ourselves wanting to blurt out strong truth in frustration, but Jesus reminds us that we are called to be as wise as serpents and as gentle as doves.

In your leadership role, whatever that might be, understand that God is always working, and that it often takes abundant time for hearts to become softened and convinced to take a particular course of action for the future.

In your patience, do not let unbiblical actions or attitudes derail the partnership conversation. Be wise and gentle, but don't withhold needed challenges and rebukes.

> Him we proclaim, warning everyone and teaching everyone with all wisdom, that we may present everyone mature in Christ. For this I toil, struggling with all his energy that he powerfully works within me. - Colossians 1:28-29

PATHWAY TO PARTNERSHIP

Partnership provides opportunities for the next generation of pastors.

About a year ago now, our church had the opportunity to partner with a declining congregation called United For Christ Church. This church was in a transition time where they had experienced some hard times; they did not have a pastor at that point and felt they were in a place of needing some direction. Through a process of meeting with them, praying, talking, and then praying some more, God led us all to partner together. United For Christ Church made the decision that they were ready for a fresh start with some new leadership. Together, we arrived at the conclusion that United For Christ Church would be replanted as a new congregation, building off of the past while looking ahead into an exciting future. This has been a wonderful journey for both churches thus far. It has not been all smooth or easy, but it has been a joy to watch God at work through this.

One of our pastoral interns was seeking where God would have him at the time this opportunity came up. Matt was interested in preaching more, so I encouraged him to go preach at this declining congregation sometime to help them and to give him opportunity to grow in his preaching. Little did we know that God would end up leading Matt and his wife to help lead this new replant as their new replanting pastor. What a gift it has been to walk with Matt as he has shepherded the replant through this transition. He has done a fantastic job depending on God through this process! Personally, I have really enjoyed just encouraging Matt, praying for him, listening to him, and helping as I can. For our church, this opportunity has given us another avenue to think beyond ourselves, to serve, and to extend Jesus' love beyond our own church and city.

God is on the move everywhere! That has been one of the key things I have been reminded of by partnering through this replant opportunity. God is not done with dying churches! Several folks have already been baptized! Community groups have been started. Outreach events have been initiated. New life has been breathed into this church! Much is yet to come there, I have no doubt. Being a part of this replant truly has been a gift.

– *Scott Iken*, Pastor of a Partner Church

Chapter 7

DETERMINING PARTNER RESPONSIBILITIES

We've established that there are many ways churches can form partnerships for the sake of the gospel, each with their varying levels of involvement and commitments. We want to pull back and give you a bigger picture of three specific levels of partnership: supporting, strategic and sending. Each level has its own characteristics and corresponding types and responsibilities, which we have just looked at in Chapter 6. We've put them all together in a graphic we call the *Partnership Pyramid* (Figure 1). The hope is that this Partnership Pyramid can serve as a tool to help you and your congregation wisely assess and discern which type of partnership would be best to pursue in this season.

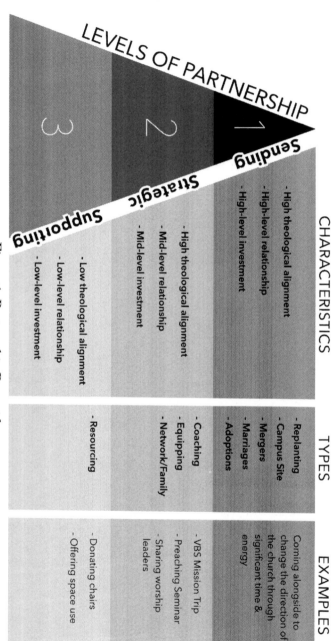

Figure 1: Partnership Pyramid

LEVELS OF PARTNERSHIP

	CHARACTERISTICS	TYPES	EXAMPLES
1 Sending	- High theological alignment - High-level relationship - High-level investment	- Replanting - Campus Site - Mergers - Marriages - Adoptions	Coming alongside to change the direction of the church through significant time & energy
2 Strategic	- High theological alignment - Mid-level relationship - Mid-level investment	- Coaching - Equipping - Network/Family	- VBS Mission Trip - Preaching Seminar - Sharing worship leaders
3 Supporting	- Low theological alignment - Low-level relationship - Low-level investment	- Resourcing	- Donating chairs - Offering space use

Here's how we've organized this in our understanding:

Levels of Partnership >> Characteristics >> Type of Partnerships >> Responsibilities

In this section we want to unpack the general responsibilities and commitments required for each level. While we can't create an exhaustive or comprehensive list exactly suited to your situation, we'll set out some guidelines that you can adopt or adapt to your context and situation. As was mentioned in the previous section you'll want to include all of this in a partnership agreement for both churches to agree to, sign and reference during the implementation of the partnership.

THE SUPPORTING CHURCH PARTNER

A supporting church is one that comes along side of a struggling or weak church (or a church plant) and offers assistance through prayer, participation and provision.

This first level of partnership is one which we believe every church could participate. The North American Mission Board has highlighted three primary commitments made by a supporting church.[5]

1. **Prayer:** Replanting and revitalizing is first and foremost a spiritual work that requires prayer. Supporting churches commit to pray for the church and those who are leading it forward.

2. **Participation:** whether it be a workday to clean, organize, repair or paint a supporting church can send people and teams to assist the struggling church accomplish more in one

or two days than it could on its own in many weeks or months.

3. **Provision**: in a church that has experienced decline for some time there are often physical facility and material needs. Be it a sound system, new chairs or tables, a supporting church can be of great practical assistance in simply providing much needed material resources. These resource and financial commitments are primarily short term and need or project-based.

As a general guide, the supporting church seeks to find and meet a need. The ability to do so is enhanced as the two churches spend time getting to know one another and developing clear lines of communication. The length of this relationship varies and can be short or long term.[6]

THE STRATEGIC CHURCH PARTNER

This relationship is formed as two churches who are of like mind (theologically and missiologically) come together to pray, think through and strategize how the struggling or weaker church can move forward with its mission of proclaiming the gospel to the community more effectively.

It may contain some or all of the elements of the supporting church level but differs in that this partnership requires more relational commitments between the leaders of both congregations and it is more long term.

This level of partnership is highly relational. Pastors, staff and lay leaders invest in coaching and equipping relationships with the struggling or weaker church on a regular basis. Here are some ways we've seen this relationship flesh itself out.

- Staff/Leaders invited to join the strategic church staff meetings regularly
- Ministry equipping and training provided by the strategic church
- One-on-one mentoring from strategic church staff and leaders
- Facilitation of strategic planning for the struggling church
- Comprehensive ministry evaluation and consultation by the strategic church

This is one of the most challenging partnership types, in that strategic partners offer counsel, wisdom and advice which may be accepted or rejected. This is a partnership that relies influence thru relationship rather than authority. It may be wise to secure some form of agreements that help set expectations for both partners so that each understands their role and responsibilities. If a strategic partner grows concerned that their assistance and suggestions are not being adequately considered or accepted, they will want to meet to discuss their concerns and consider how they may realign their expectations or disengage or end the partnership.

THE SENDING CHURCH PARTNER

A sending church accepts responsibility for a church replant until it is self-sustaining, self-governing and self-propagating. Serving a church replant as a sending church is an incredible opportunity; it represents the highest level of involvement a congregation can make in the work of replanting. The North American Mission Board has established some best practices for those making the commitment to be a sending church.[7] These are focused on church planting specifically, but there is valuable cross-application for those engaging with a church replant.

In most cases the sending church assumes complete directional leadership of the congregation that is being replanted and it is involved in finding, calling, assessing and coaching the newly called replanter. The struggling church agrees to accept directional leadership by congregational vote or affirmation.

This partnership is often resource taxing for the sending church partner. In assuming responsibility, they take on financial and administrative responsibilities, as well as assisting in facility upgrades and leadership during the transition as the church awaits the arrival of a qualified and called replanter. Once a replanter is called, the sending church often underwrites a portion of the salary and benefits for the replanter for an agreed-upon period of time.

We recommend that churches consider carefully their readiness to become a sending church partner for a replant as was outlined in Chapter 3.

THE ROLE OF THE REPLANT CHURCH

To be clear, we see partnership as a two-way relationship. The stronger church and the struggling church both must make commitments for any partnership to work out well. Occasionally there are elements in the partnership that create tension (understandably so). With one church coming from a place of strength and the other from a place of weakness, there are bound to be sensitivities and perspectives that can contribute to the creation of conflict or misunderstanding.

A struggling church can develop feelings of inferiority and the stronger partnering church can come across as better or superior. Acknowledging this upfront can go a long way in setting the stage for helpful and healthy conversations that lead both partners forward.

Below are necessary and healthy commitments to be made by a church agreeing to receiving partnership or being replanted.

- We acknowledge that our trends (attendance, finances, baptisms, etc.) demonstrate that our congregation is not growing and/or healthy.
- We acknowledge that our congregation may lack the energy, experience and knowledge required to reach our community.
- Therefore, we acknowledge that our church is in need of partnership.
- We agree to humbly evaluate everything in our church.
- We commit to hold our tradition, programs and style of ministry loosely, and are open to changing these things.
- We agree to receive help from a partner church and welcome their leadership.
- We believe that God is not done with our church and that in the days to come, it may look very different than it does now.
- We commit to pray and work together with our partner church in seeking the future that God has for us.
- We commit to support our leaders and work to maintain unity in the body as we become who God is calling us to be as a church.
- If, as an individual member, I cannot keep the commitments above, I will willingly leave this fellowship and unite with one where I can worship and serve with all joy and unity.

A CLOSING WORD

We believe we've made a solid case for the value and biblical mandate for partnership between churches. This partnership is for God's glory and the good of the communities that need to hear the gospel and see it lived out in their midst. And with our effort to do so, we want to be very clear: *partnering with a sister church can be challenging.* It requires humility, patience, submission and surrender. Most congregations struggle to live these out as a single autonomous congregation by themselves. The next section will take a look at some of the reasons partnerships struggle and sometimes fail.

PATHWAY TO PARTNERSHIP

Partnership helps congregations live on mission.

Getting a congregation outside the four walls of their building and living on mission is a goal of any gospel-centered church. In moving outside the walls of the church and into the community, they experience the reality that they were created for the joy of Matthew 28:19, "Go therefore and make disciples of all nations, baptizing them in the name of the Father, the Son and the Holy Spirit"! How exciting it is to see the lights come on within individuals as they begin to experience the reality that Matthew 28:19 isn't simply one conversation with a stranger, but rather a life on mission of loving, caring and building trust with the lost and broken in the community. This is the life on mission every church replanter is striving to create within a replant.

Partnering with a church replant is one of the easiest way to experience people living out the gospel on a daily basis. A replanting pastor is transitioning the existing church culture to one that lives on mission to reach those far from Christ in their community. The wonderful part of this for a partner congregation is that in many cases a church replant is only a few hours drive from their church. They don't have to go to a foreign country to experience life on mission. Instead of a partner congregation having to raise thousands of dollars to secure airfare to a foreign country once a year, multiple trips, involving many more people throughout the year, can be involved in hands-on partnership with a replant. Not only is this more affordable and allows for more people to experience mission in a new way, but remaining funds can even go to the church replant for future outreach.

Let me share one of the ways we have seen partnership serve as a win-win for both the replant and a partner church. For many replants, the majority of the remaining, legacy members of the church are very tired and have not experienced the thrill of living on mission in their community for years. This replant needs the youth, excitement, confidence, and missional passion that a partner church can provide. At the same time, the sweet saints from the replant can pour godly wisdom, love and care into the lives of those from a partner church who may be younger and in need of mentoring and friendship from those of older generations. The body of Christ is always better together! We need one another, young and old. Partnership allows each of our congregations to grow and mature, learning from one another as we become more of what Jesus desires us to be.

— *Jeff Declue*, Replanting Pastor

PART TWO
DISCUSSION QUESTIONS

Defining the Partner Relationship

1. Why do we believe God is leading us to consider partnering together for the Gospel?

2. How will our church contribute to the new partnership? What assets and strengths are we bringing to the potential partnership?

3. How will our congregation be involved in this partnership process?

4. Who will our leaders be accountable to as decision makers in this process?

5. How will we resolve conflict and disagreements that arise with the other church? How can we work to minimize potential conflict from the start?

6. Define the type of partnership that would serve both congregations best. See Chapter 6.

7. How will we practice humility in our partnership together? As the Partner Church? As the Replant?

For the Replant:

- What level of partnership would help our church become healthy, vibrant and missional once again?

- What level of partnership are we open to receiving?

- What would that level of partnership require of us in terms of acceptance, change and accountability?

For the Partner Church:

- What level of partnership are we ready, willing and able to commit to right now?

- Are we willing to walk the distance with a church understanding that partnership is costly?

- What would that level of partnership require of us in terms of commitment, resources (people, finances, leadership), and patience.

PART 3

CREATING
THRIVING PARTNERSHIPS

Chapter 8

WHY PARTNERSHIPS STRUGGLE

One of the joys in pastoring a local congregation is being asked to perform wedding ceremonies. Before I agree to officiate a ceremony, my wife and I secure a commitment from the couple to spend several months doing premarital preparation. Sessions cover many topics like communication, family history, finances, intimacy and conflict resolution. One of the most important sessions we lead couples through is dealing with expectations.

Just this past week we were meeting with a couple, for whom we did not do premarital counseling, and the husband made this comment; "I guess since we've been married seven years it's probably time to talk about expectations." We all had a good laugh, but the previous six years for them have been filled with hurt, resentment and anger, all of which brought them to the brink of divorce. Much of their struggle could have been avoided by simply talking through as many things as they could prior to their wedding.

Conflict is inherent to every relationship that has ever, church partnerships included. Like couples who date, get engaged and head toward marriage, churches who explore partnerships have unexpressed expectations and historical baggage. These create conflict and can potentially derail good partnerships. Let's take a look at some of the reasons behind the struggle churches have in partnering together.

PARTNERSHIPS STRUGGLE FROM LACK OF CLARITY

What is clear to a sending, supporting or strategic church may not clear to the struggling church receiving help. For example, when both partners say they want to reach people with the Gospel, see them saved and become part of life of the church, how does one know if they are talking about the same people?

In some settings where a struggling church no longer reflects the community around them in age or demographic, the people likely to be reached in this setting are vastly different than those who drive in from other locations to gather for worship on Sunday. Reaching people may be understood by the legacy members to reach people who look like them or reflect the people who were part of the church in its heyday. The partner church likely understands that people likely to be reached are those who are in the immediate area. In some cases, we've encountered actually reaching people in the immediate community in which the church is situated can strangely spark unanticipated conflict.

Gaining extreme clarity requires many conversations on various topics, and it requires churches to *write out just about everything,* and then do the important work of checking again for clarity.

Here are some of the things you'll want to ensure both partners have clarity regarding:

- **Expectations and Roles:** How decisions will be made, what is happening, what will happen, who is doing what and who is accountable to whom.

- **Facilities:** Will they remain as is or will they be remodeled? Who will oversee access and care of the building, and what groups will continue to meet in the building?

- **Membership:** One of the most sensitive topics in church partnerships deals with how legacy members will become part of the new church. It is easy to declare that all historical members will need to enter into the new membership process and it may be right to do so—yet it's important to realize the impact that process may have on those who were part of the church from its founding days.

- **Holidays and Special Services:** We recommend review of both church calendars in order to determine what a joint calendar should look like.

- **Worship Style:** When and where possible, we recommend that the partnering church send a worship team to lead services for the struggling church. This helps bring about awareness and bridge the gap between congregations. It is important to take into account style, volume and music selections that allow both congregations to participate enthusiastically. This sets the stage for what musical worship could look like going forward.

- **Existing/New Ministries:** As the two churches join together, it will be important to determine which ministries will continue or cease, and which ones will remain. It is often possible to find common ground to begin or merge existing ministries and allow long standing ones remain.

- **Theological Distinctions:** We are consistently surprised at the level of assumption that takes place in one of the most critical areas of a church's life—doctrine. Churches from the same denomination are generally like-minded in primary beliefs, but may have differences that require conversation, instruction and working toward agreement. Matters of membership, baptism, charismatic gifts, The Lord's supper, qualifications and processes for approval and selection of deacons and elders/pastors can vary widely. In some cases, struggling churches have not given careful thought to these matters.

- **Finances:** It is important for both churches to discuss the method of receiving offerings, the oversight and disbursements of funds, special offerings, purchasing policies, staff salaries and benefits.

- **Baggage/Culture:** Every church has a history and churches who partner together inherit each other's histories. In many ways, this can be very positive and good, yet at times historic hurts create dysfunctional culture that requires significant relational leadership and time to overcome. Fear and hesitancy and an overabundance of caution can't be resolved by a compelling vision or impatient leadership. Each church partner will want to do as much self-critical evaluation as possible to understand its history, culture and any baggage it is bringing to the partnership.

- **Partnerships Struggle for Lack of Relationship:** One of the defining characteristics of a smaller and perhaps struggling church is that it is highly relational (and perhaps in a dysfunctional way). In such an environment, everyone may know or feel the need to know what is going on and have a say in that as well. A new partnership will lead to changes in the way a church does "church." Fewer people may be "in the know." In many cases if not, all these changes are not only necessary, they will be helpful and are even biblical. This still may not lead to enthusiastic acceptance by the church receiving partnership.

Churches partnering together will need to spend time building relationships, not just doing tasks or seeking to fulfill the mission. This particularly can be a difficult transition for some partnering churches who are used to moving fast, making decisions quickly and moving toward implementation immediately. If the leadership and care of the partnership has been entrusted to someone from the stronger church who feels this is an additional assignment or obligation, we believe conflict and struggle will almost be guaranteed. If at all possible, we recommend that this developing partnership become the primary responsibility for a staff lead or team for a season and that they be tasked with nothing aside from caring for the partnering church and leading well.

Churches in the lead position will create tension when they are:

- Committed to tasks rather than relationships
- Committed to results rather than discipleship
- Committed to the weekend rather than entire week

The Apostle Paul serves as a great model for us. As a bold apologist and evangelist, we might expect that he would possess a gruff get it done demeanor, but scripture actually shows that he had a very tender and compassionate side.

> We cared so much for you that we were pleased to share with you not only the gospel of God but also our own lives, because you had become dear to us. - 1 Thessalonians 2:8

PARTNERSHIPS STRUGGLE FROM A LACK OF HUMILITY

One of the best definitions of humility I've ever heard comes from Author and Pastor Tim Keller. He writes; "The essence of gospel-humility is not thinking more of myself or thinking less of myself, it is thinking of myself less."[8]

Churches can develop great partnerships through humility. Here are some ways that might express itself in the life of a stronger or weaker/struggling church:

Not Thinking More of Our Church

- That our church (the stronger church) has all the right answers.
- That our church (the weaker/struggling church) has traditions that must be maintained.
- That our church (the stronger church) has come to the rescue.
- That our church (the weaker/struggling church) reserves the right to veto all decisions.

Not Thinking Less of our Church

- We (the weaker/struggling church) have nothing to offer this partnership.
- We (the weaker/struggling church) have failed in ministry and is being judged.
- We (the weaker/struggling church) aren't really wanted in this partnership.
- We (the weaker/struggling church) and our members can now just sit back and let others serve.

Thinking of Our Church Less

- Our church (the stronger church) can learn from these faithful saints.
- Our church (the weaker/struggling) can learn how to reach the community from our new partner church.
- Our church (the stronger church) can honor and celebrate the history of what God has done in our new partner church.
- Our church (the weaker/struggling church) can love the new incoming families and children more than we love our history, traditions and culture.

PARTNERSHIPS STRUGGLE FROM UNRESOLVED CONFLICT

Every single partnership that develops between churches will experience conflict at some point along the way. Rather than viewing conflict as a bad thing, we see it as one of the signs that God is doing something good in the body.

Paul writing to the Christians in Corinth indicates that his trip to visit them will be delayed because two reasons: a wide door of ministry has opened before him, and because there are many adversaries.[9]

Today pastors and leaders may not see the presence of adversaries or conflict as a reason to stay, but as a reason to leave. When conflict occurs, especially conflict over non-essential and non-biblical matters of preference, God is working to bring the church toward maturity. It's not a time to leave but *stay*. Some may respond not as wise shepherds, but as foolish ones, berating the sheep or abandoning the flock.

While the presence of conflict is good, the presence of unresolved conflict is dangerous and even deadly to the unity of the body.

Paul urges us:

> I therefore, a prisoner for the Lord, urge you to walk in a manner worthy of the calling to which you have been called, with all humility and gentleness, with patience, bearing with one another in love, eager to maintain the unity of the Spirit in the bond of peace. - Ephesians 4:1-3

As the partnership progresses, we recommend clear and compelling teaching on the sins of gossip and slander and instruct the body on resolving conflict according to Matthew 18. 1 Timothy 5:19 is a helpful passage on how to handle concerns or questions about pastors/elders according to.

PARTNERSHIPS STRUGGLE WHEN COMMITMENTS ARE ABANDONED

Scripture contains abundant examples of people being reminded of the promises of God—both the covenants he has made with them, and the covenants they have made with him. I'm convinced one of the reasons we see this over and over is that leaders and people forget the commitments they make to God and one another.

Let's agree that partnership agreements between churches do not rise to the level of God's law, but they are important in that churches are agreeing *before* God to commit to one another as they become a new church body for his glory.

It's one thing to forget the details of a commitment made, and an entirely different matter to know and then abandon them. We've seen both in partnerships. Here are some things we have found helpful to keep commitments before the people.

- **Read the Partnership Commitments:** Take the time to remind everyone to what both partners have committed. This can be done in members meetings, at prayer gatherings, in bible study classes and leaders meetings.

- **Post the Partnership Commitments:** Create a space where the documents of the covenants and commitments can be viewed and read by those who gather for worship. Adding pictures of both churches, and their congregants creates a visual display of the two coming together and becoming one body.

- **Provide Copies of the Partnership Commitments:** Getting documents in the hands of church members forming this partnership is critical. It allows members to read and re-read the specifics of the partnership being formed. This can be especially helpful for older members and those who process information from meetings over time. Including information on how questions can be asked and answered creates an avenue for greater unity and trust.

MORE COMMON ROADBLOCKS TO PARTNERSHIP

The road to developing partnerships between churches is a winding one, it may have blind corners or potholes. It also may have some roadblocks along the way. These are some of the more common ones we encounter in working with churches who partner together.

- **Lack of Trust:** Most often the struggling church has spent the bulk of its emotional and spiritual energy on preservation and protection. Years of decline and a scarcity mentality create an environment where almost everything can be viewed as a threat to the life and future of the church. Building trust takes time and the stronger church seeking to partner will do well to create a relationship of trust by taking intentional relational steps.

- **Unclear Vision:** In order to bring both churches into a healthy and vibrant partnership, it is important to communicate a clear picture of God's preferred future. This is not simply communicating logistical and strategic details. *Vision captures the hearts and enlarges the view of the people of God.* It inspires and calls people to believe more, and pursue that expanded belief with passion and energy. A clear vision goes a long way to diminish the elevation of personal preferences because it calls the body to something greater than the promotion of self.

- **Lacking a Strategic Plan:** Vision is great, but if you don't have a strategic plan to accomplish that vision, then it's just talk and it will lead to people becoming frustrated and hurt (which could ultimately lead to their departure). Visionaries need to partner with people who can work to make that vision a reality. Communicate vision, but also communicate action plans. Communicate and display these steps in similar ways to the vision.

- **Poor Communication:** A pastor I served with gave me sage advice when he said, "People are down on what are not up on." Many problems can be remedied by simply providing information. It is often true that struggling congregations have more developed person-to-person lines of communication than stronger churches. Healthier churches have high levels of trust and are savvy in electronic communication, and are able to find and ask for the information they want to have. As partnerships progress, strong communication of vision and the strategic plan should be disseminated through multiple lines of communication: emails, mail, bulletin, announcements, leaders and members meetings and preaching.

- **Failing to Follow Through:** Sometimes the road toward partnership may require a course correction or even a stop-down. It is important when plans change or are delayed that this be communicated to both churches. When a promise isn't kept or a strategic action not taken, people experience a gap in what they expect and what they experience. Mistrust, suspicion and doubt can occupy that gap. So follow through, keep commitments, and when they can't, communicate why.

Managing and developing partnerships between churches can be exhausting work, but the results can have exponential impact for the Gospel. We encourage you to roll up your selves and do the work that is required in partnering well for the glory of God and the good of the community.

PATHWAY TO PARTNERSHIP

Partnership helps provide practical help to struggling churches.

Nampa First Southern Baptist Church was founded in partnership by a local pastor in a neighboring town in 1957. Over the first several decades, our church in turn helped to support several missions and churches throughout the region. By the turn of the century, however, the church found itself at the center of significant population growth that came with a changing culture. Eventually, this led to a decline in relevancy and significance in the community. In the spring of 2016, the church experienced significant turmoil in leadership and visionary direction, which resulted in struggling membership and a lack of resources. Remaining leaders knew the church must significantly change in order to be a relevant gospel force in our community. The trouble was we had no idea what that looked like or how to do it.

We were eventually connected to a congregation that had a passion to help declining churches like ours. This church brought immediate encouragement to our congregation who was growing tired. They themselves had walked the path we now looked down, bringing a wealth of understanding and knowledge on replanting, along with the basics of discipleship and missional living. Together, we soon sensed that the best thing we could do for our church was to be replanted as a new congregation. When we decided to replant with this other congregation (our sending church), our church was immediately provided a springboard of vision, mission, values, and ministry philosophy. We were given help with tangible things like branding, print and electronic media, experience with modern audio/visual and children's ministry practices. They helped identify a replanting pastor who was excited and passionate about the work to be done in a church like ours. The effort became a vehicle to plant a flag in the ground and start a new work which fostered additional partnerships with local churches and organizations that are proving invaluable.

I passionately believe we need more churches that are willing to invest in and encourage one another; the nominal church in America may not be able to survive on its own, but we are truly better together if we will only embrace radical cooperation for the fame of His name!

– Jon Kempf, Member of a new Replant

Chapter 8

THE FIVE PILLARS OF EFFECTIVE PARTNERSHIP

Why is it that some church partnerships thrive while others don't?

This is a question we have given a lot of thought to. Specifically regarding partnerships with replanted congregations, what is it that separate effective and successful partnerships from those that flounder?

In this chapter, we want to lay out the five ingredients that stand out in every thriving partnership. These are things that are consistently present in church partnerships that are healthy, joy-filled, and increasingly marked by trust and intimacy over the long haul. We simply refer to these as the five pillars of effective partnership.

PILLAR 1: TIME TOGETHER

An important first step in building the trust needed for partnership is by simply spending time with one another. There is nothing that replaces quality time together. Friendship is built with time—time encouraging one another, praying for one another, serving together. Time dreaming together about Kingdom ministry. Time together is critical to healthy partnership.

If partner churches are not located in close proximity to one another, that is ok. One of the great blessings of technology is that it allows for quality relationships to be developed between congregations by way of consistent, regularly scheduled phone or video calls. In these calls, churches should seek to ask good questions and listen to one another well. They should dream together and pray for one another. The more time spent in intentional conversation and prayer with each other, the closer you grow as partners in the Gospel. The ideal partnership will be marked by a combination of phone and video call interaction, as well as "in person" group visits.

I can remember with one of our first church replants, spending a day driving around town with one of the congregation's core leaders who was a police officer. I wanted him to know that we loved him and we loved their church. That we desired to be a helpful partner with their congregation. It was an honor as he drove me around town, gave me a tour of the police station where he worked, and told me all kinds of stories about being a cop in Denver. We talked about the Lord and his faithfulness in our lives and in the lives of those in his church. We laughed together and we praised God together. I will never forget it, and I'm guessing he won't either. It was such a blessing to spend this day together. The Lord united our hearts as friends in a unique way that day. Trust was built. And this trust served as the foundation for our churches moving forward together as partners in ministry.

PILLAR 2: EXCESSIVE ENCOURAGEMENT

Encouragement is powerful. Who doesn't love to be encouraged? We are commanded all throughout Scripture to encourage one another, and for good reason—life is hard. It is easy to become discouraged for all kinds of reasons. Many folks in dying churches are discouraged as they see the congregation they love so much decline and begin to face the prospect of closed doors. Even as they move toward revitalization as a replant, one of the most powerful ways to build trust with a church like this is to encourage them! Encourage them and help them see some of the ways that God is alive and at work in their church. Encourage them by helping them to imagine all that God desires to do in and through them in the future. Encourage them by identifying evidences of God's grace in their lives. A new perspective can change a lot. Encouragement can help with this—it is love spoken. A new replant needs a lot of love and encouragement. Effective partnership is marked by this kind of excessive, Christ-like encouragement.

PILLAR 3: FAITHFUL COMMITMENT

A great pastor friend of mine who I was blessed to serve under as a youth pastor for many years, Deral Schrom, had a saying he would share with me regularly. "Stay steady." What Deral meant by this phrase was simply, *be faithful. Be consistent. Be a man of your word. Be steady, not flaky*. I think of Deral's words often. Throughout a partnership, there are many meetings, conversations, email interactions and phone calls that must happen between the replant and the partner church. Because of this, there are many opportunities to prove either your steadiness or your flakiness to one another. A church and its leaders have an opportunity to win the trust of the other congregation through this partnership process as they follow through on commitments that have been made. Of course, churches also have the opportunity to lose trust if they fail to follow through on commitments that have been made. Be steady by following through on commitments you make in this church partnership.

PILLAR 4: CLEAR COMMUNICATION

When it comes to matters in any church, you can never over-communicate. I'm convinced that under-communication is the cause for so many divisions and unnecessary conflicts in congregations. Good, clear communication is absolutely key to growing a healthy and unified church. The same is true when it comes to church partnership.

Assuring that your communication is clear takes intentionality. It means going overboard to make sure everyone who needs to be in the loop actually is. Don't assume anything—ever. Don't assume that just because you spent an hour explaining the implications of partnership to the core leaders of your congregation that they completely understand what this will actually entail for them. The same is true for the other congregation. Why? Because effective church partnership is probably a new thing for many in both congregations. And with anything that is new in the church, it takes consistent, clear communication over and over again.

This isn't an indictment against anyone's intellect or ability to comprehend what is involved with partnership; it is simply a realistic perspective on who we are as humans. It might also be a case of selective listening, which we can all fall into. We think we understand things when we really don't, or we understand some aspects but not others. We also quickly forget things we hear. When it comes to the conversation about partnership, there will be some who understand and there will be some who don't, or at least don't fully get it. Because of this, we need to over-communicate. You may need to utilize multiple forms of communication. Phone calls, emails, text messages, home visits, whatever it takes—clear communication is absolutely essential. Remember, in-person, face-to-face communication is always best.

PILLAR 5: GRACE-FILLED PATIENCE

As I've mentioned several times already: The process of partnership takes time. Effective partnership takes many conversations, time spent together and genuine trust that serves as the foundation for the entire process. Because of this, grace-filled patience must be practiced toward one another as congregations and as brothers and sisters in Christ.

The Lord is sovereign in all things. He is sovereign over our lives, over the world, and over this partnership process. This should give us great peace and cause us to practice prayerful patience as we seek to move forward with wisdom, love and unity. We want to honor God in the process by not getting ahead of him. We must ask God to guide and lead us every step of the way. We must seek His face in prayerful dependence on His Spirit to show us the way He wants us to go, asking him to give both congregations a supernatural unity that can only come from the Spirit. We must pray that the Lord's will would be done in His perfect timing and that we would remain prayerfully patient through it all.

PATHWAY TO PATHWAY PARTNERSHIP

Partnership helps fuel joy in the heart of Replanters.

As children of God, we are called into relationship with other believers through the local church. In Scripture, the idea of a Lone Ranger Christian is completely absent. We are to be part of a body that has many parts but is united as one (Romans 12:3-5). In the same way, churches that are being replanted cannot function in a healthy manner as an island while seeking to do Kingdom work. We need one another for encouragement, mutual building-up, and strength in our weaknesses. I have personally seen the crucial, indispensable help that comes by partnering with other churches as our church is being replanted.

The replant I pastor has had the blessing of partnering with several churches during our first year. The legacy members of the church are mostly in their 70's, 80's, and 90's which made initial efforts to push out into the community with outreach projects difficult. Yet, through partnering churches, in our first year we were able to put on block parties, parking lot outreaches, service projects in the community, a sports camp in a local park, and canvasing in our neighborhood. Without this help we would never have been able to begin again to love and serve our community for the sake of Jesus as we seek to make Him non-ignorable!

Replanting can be a lonely and difficult uphill climb but taking that hike hand in hand with other churches and pastors enables one to press on well. The prayer, financial, logistical and mentoring support that an established church can give to a replanting church should never be underestimated. Without the help we have had in these areas, I am sure that I would have found myself feeling isolated, defeated, and at a great loss as to how to navigate the challenges of replanting. Partnering churches and pastors have been agents of God's grace to me to enable me to joyfully serve through the challenges and heartache that have accompanied the replanting process.

– *Dave Herre,* Replanting Pastor

Chapter 10

PRACTICAL STRATEGIES:
Partnering with a Replant

One of the main reasons why some church replants fail within the first few years is because they are attempting to do it all alone. As we have tried our best to argue throughout this book, just as there is no such thing as a lone ranger Christian, there is no such thing as a lone ranger church. As followers of Jesus need other followers of Jesus to pray for them, counsel, teach, and encourage them, churches also need these very same things from other churches. Replanted congregations desperately need continual encouragement, cooperation and assistance from partner churches.

There are many different ways a partner church can come alongside a replant to encourage and serve them for the long haul. This long-term partner relationship is absolutely vital to the health and growth of this new church. But it also takes great intentionality to make it happen. Here are some of the most important and practical ways this kind of intentional, radical cooperation and partnership can look.

LEADERSHIP DEVELOPMENT

One of the greatest needs the replant will have is the training of leaders in the church. This might include the training of deacons and new elders, or the training of a variety of ministry team leaders (such as the greeting and hospitality team). A partner church has resources and experienced leaders who can help train these individuals. Not only will it allow your people the excitement and privilege of connecting with people from the replant on a personal level, your investment in these leaders will help strengthen the replant and help assure that their leadership is solid and well-equipped for effective ministry in the future.

FINANCES

Typically it takes quite some time to put together an excellent finance team in a church, and a replant is no exception. This is another way a partner church can serve this congregation—helping the replant figure out their current financial situation, develop new systems of accountability, put together strategies for recording and depositing offerings, and design a new budget for the church are all ways a partner church can serve the replant in financial matters.

VOLUNTEER TEAMS

Regularly sending volunteer teams from a partner church to help the new congregation is sure way to maintain close relationship.

It is a joy for folks in the partner church to take a Sunday to worship with and serve alongside their brothers and sisters in the replant. Likewise, it is a great blessing for the pastor and members of the replant to have groups come and serve. Maintaining close relationship between the two churches is crucial. This intentional and ongoing sending of teams is a strategic way to assure that the new congregation feels loved and supported continually by a partner church.

SHARING PRINTED MATERIALS

An easy way a partner church can help the replant out weekly is in sharing and printing resources for the new congregation. For example, our church designs and prints out the weekly bulletin for each of our replants. This not only helps with cost and time, but it allows the replant to have a great looking bulletin they may not otherwise be able to produce on their own.

WEBSITE

In this day and age, the website is the first place the large majority of people look to find out about a new church. Most replants do not have the funds and resources to design and run an up-to-date website. This should be a primary way a partner church helps serve the replant. Do whatever it takes to help the replant have an excellent website. If that means designing it, paying for it and helping to run it, serve this new church through helping them with their website.

GRAPHIC DESIGN

Most likely, a partner church has access to graphics and design software that is visually appealing to those both inside and outside the church. Most replants do not have access to these same resources. Giving them free usage of any and all graphics used by the partner church will allow them to have a level of quality in their printed materials that most small churches are unable to afford or develop.

MARKETING AND SIGNAGE

As this new replant is preparing to launch, it is important for a partner church to help with marketing and new signage both throughout the inside and outside of the church. Helping to pay for an updated sign for the church is a huge blessing, and the neighborhood will take notice! Help to design and pay for marketing materials that communicate to the community a new church will be launching. Flyers, door hangers, ads on Facebook or in the local newspaper are all effective means to help get the word out and let folks in the community know you want them to be part of this congregation.

WORSHIP MUSIC

Weekly worship music is an important component in helping the replant create a God-honoring, edifying worship gathering. There are many ways a partner congregation can help in this area. Sending musicians to help lead services, making connections with other local churches who might have musicians who can help periodically, or perhaps paying for a very part-time worship leader in the replant. The bottom line is that a partner church should be eager to come alongside this newly replanted congregation to help them develop a quality worship experience.

YOUTH AND CHILDREN'S MINISTRY RESOURCES

There typically is a great need for a new approach and strategy in children's and youth ministry for a small replant. At the same time, it can be a major challenge if there are few people to help lead these ministries. A partner church can help by sharing access to curriculum, teachers training resources, policy and procedure documents, VBS materials, along with volunteers who can help out on a weekend. All of these can help a small replant enjoy the same level of ministry excellence that you would typically find in a larger church. This is extremely helpful as they seek to reach new families in the community.

FINDING OTHER PARTNER CHURCHES

Just like new church plants, replants need multiple partner churches to come alongside them for encouragement, prayer support, financial support, and other forms of help and assistance. It takes a great deal of time and energy to form relationships of trust with pastors and leaders of potential partner churches. As a result, it can be difficult for a replanting pastor and the few leaders in the replant to find these partner churches on their own. Typically, the time and energy needed to find partner churches is better spent focusing on the health and growth of this newly replanted congregation. As a partner church, your congregation can be a huge help in this by reaching out to denominational leaders and other pastors and churches, casting vision and inviting them to support the ministry. I believe there are many healthy churches that would love to partner with a new replant if only they were aware of the needs. Your church can help immensely with spreading the word and seeking additional partnership on behalf of the replant from these congregations.

OFFICE ADMINISTRATIVE HELP

One of the most burdensome aspects of replanting for many replanters is having to oversee administrative tasks that are often carried out by an administrative assistant in a larger church. Time and energy that could be spent building relationships with those in the congregation and community can get drowned out by the pressing demands of producing the bulletin or making copies for Sunday School teachers. A partner church can help tremendously in this area by taking care of some of these needs. Making copies or bulletins, gathering new information on members and visitors, or helping oversee the scheduling of events and building usage, are some ways a partner church can help with administrative needs.

PRAYER SUPPORT

Newly replanted congregations are in great need of faithful prayer support. Here is a list of twelve specific ways partner churches can pray for both the replanter and his family, as well as the replant as a congregation. It would be worthwhile to brainstorm creative ways you can equip and encourage people in the partner church to pray for these twelve things on a regular and consistent basis.

12 Prayers for a Replant

1. Pray for replant and its leaders to keep their eyes on God and not take a step apart from God's leading.

2. Pray for courage and boldness to go where the Lord leads.

3. Pray for humility before the Lord and people, prioritizing the raising up of other leaders.

4. Pray for the replant and its leaders to not rely on their own strength, but trust in the Lord's strength.

5. Pray for a deep heart of love for those leading this new replant.

6. Pray for the health of marriages and families in the congregation.

7. Pray for the replant and its leaders to walk worthy of the calling God has placed on their lives.

8. Pray for the replanter to preach the Word and the Gospel boldly.

9. Pray for God to destroy idols in the hearts of the leaders and of those in the congregation.

10. Pray for God-honoring unity in the congregation.

11. Pray the replant and its leaders will do whatever it takes to reach the lost.

12. Pray for the making of disciples who make disciples in and through the replant.

7 ways a replant can communicate with church partners

Some of the best church planting advice I ever received had nothing to do with preaching, evangelism, or budgets. It was a statement made during our church planting boot camp while our replanting team skyped with a fellow church planter serving in Cleveland, Ohio. He said that, from his experience, "You cannot over-communicate with your prayer partners and supporters.

This powerful statement resonated with me and shaped our vision as we began our journey of church planting. We are now just over two years into our replant, and we have seen tremendous fruit from strong communication with our partners. Here are seven ways we found to strengthen communication with our partners.

1. **Send an initial letter** detailing the vision and goals of your replant. Before we started replanting, our team sent out hundreds of letters to potential partners, detailing our vision and goals. We eventually were blessed to have about 20 financial sponsors and more than 250 prayer partners. This helped strengthen communication as it gave us the base of who we knew we could communicate with and trust to pray for us.

2. **Send newsletters.** Newsletters have been the most rewarding part of our communication with our partners. We share stories of God's goodness and faithfulness, as well as our struggles and concerns. We hear from so many of our partners how blessed they are to read the stories of what God is doing at Crosspoint. Not only that, but as we write the newsletters, we are blessed to think through God's faithfulness at Crosspoint. As you write newsletters, share victory stories, upcoming events, and specific examples of God's faithfulness at your replant. Believe me, it is a fruitful task.

3. **Share specific prayer requests and praises.** On the last page of our newsletter, we have a detailed list of specific prayer concerns. We also share stories of how God has been faithful to answer prayer. We hear from our partners of how they are encouraged to know how to pray, as well as to see prayers God has answered. This gives us great confidence as we face tasks we think are very difficult. We know we have hundreds of people praying for us and lifting us up to the Father.

4. **Share pictures.** I can't think of a time in my life that someone has not enjoyed looking at pictures. When you share pictures with your partners, they will be able to not only read about what God is doing, but they will see it as well. The pictures you share truly are "worth a thousand words." What you can't say in so many words in your newsletter, you can say in one picture. We share pictures of baptisms, events, worship services, etc. It is just a fun way for partners to get excited about what God is doing. Our partners are constantly telling us that they love to see the pictures!

5. **Say thank you.** We make sure to always say "Thank you!" to our financial partners and prayer partners. This might be in the newsletter itself, or sometimes we put in a separate note. It is a simple way your partners know they are not just a name on a piece of paper, but that you are thankful for them personally.

6. **Invest in a paid website.** Our church website has been a fantastic tool for communication. While the initial cost of the website was large, it has paid off in great ways. Through the website, our partners learn about upcoming events and sermon series, see pictures, and more. A wonderful piece of advice we received about the website was to put our church address on each page, so when a Google search is conducted for churches in our area, ours would be one of the first to pop up. When we took this advice, our website went from page 3 of the search results to the top of page 1. This proved to be another great way to communicate with our people.

7. **Use social media to your advantage.** We make sure to post a lot of information on our church Facebook page and Twitter feed. This allows our partners to see daily and weekly updates of what God is doing.

Sometimes, the thought of writing newsletters, sharing prayer concerns, and keeping up on social media can seem like a daunting task that you may not feel like doing. However, it is well worth it and will be very fruitful in replanting ministry.

When you don't feel like writing that 20th newsletter or posting another Facebook item, remember that you can never over-communicate with your partners. In the end, God will receive the glory and people will know how to pray and support the work you are doing in replanting.

Dan Conrades
Replant Pastor of Crosspoint Church
Richmond, IN

PATHWAY TO PARTNERSHIP

Partnership spreads the fame of Jesus!

This last fall our church had the chance to partner with a newly replanted church in Deer Trail, Colorado, forty-five miles east of the Denver metro area where our congregation is located. On Sunday, September 3rd, we canceled our normal Sunday gathering in Aurora to help this new replant prepare for their official launch by helping with their Sunday Gathering, fixing up their building, and canvasing the community of Deer Trail to spread the word about the church's official launch the following Sunday. This incredible opportunity turned out to be a huge blessing for our church and here are three reasons why.

First, partnering with this new replant was a blessing for our church because it helped us further accomplish our vision of making Jesus non-ignorable. We may be a small church but we have a huge goal: we want to see our city and our world transformed by Jesus. We believe that we will accomplish this goal not by becoming a big church ourselves but rather, that we would be a church that radically and generously gives people and resources to help plant and replant churches. We believe that when we partner with other churches we collectively make a greater impact for God's kingdom than we would be able to alone.

Second, partnering with a replant was a blessing for our congregation because partnering together communicated to our church that we are not the center of our universe, God is. We do not want to be about making a name for ourselves in Aurora, rather we want to be about making much of Jesus. What better way to communicate this truth to our people than to close our church doors one Sunday and go serve another like-minded church replant outside our city? As churches, I believe it is very easy to give into the lie that church is about us. It is about our building, our budget, our size; in short it is about our name. This was a way for us to push against these cultural values and for us to remember the bigger story God is telling through small churches like ours across our state.

Third and finally, partnering with a replant was a blessing to our church because it is a joy to give our lives away for the good of others. As Paul reminds us in Acts 20, "it is better to give than to receive." Giving naturally produces joy and joy is always a blessing, especially as we work together with others towards the same ultimate purpose of making Jesus famous. Church replanting can be difficult and it was an incredible gift to us to be able to come alongside of our friends in Deer Trail and show them how much we love and value them and the work they are doing to love their community to Jesus.

– *Luke Blaine*, **Pastor of a Partner Church**

Chapter 11

PRACTICAL STRATEGIES:
Partnering with a Replanter & His Family

Healthy healthiest families are all about commitment to one another—long haul commitment. A partner church and a replant need to view one another as family, (because you are). You are connected to one another as part of the family of God. This means through good times and bad times, mountain tops and valleys, the best partners seek to be there for one another. While this is true when it comes to partnering with the replant congregation itself, this is also true when it comes to partnering with the replanting pastor and his family, who have been called to lead this replant.

Why is this intentional relationship of love and care is so crucial? Consider the following three reasons why long-haul partnership with a replanter and his family is essential, not only to their health, but the health of the replant itself.

REASON 1: REPLANTING CAN BE DISCOURAGING.

Replanting is not for everyone. It takes a particular gift mix and a clear calling from the Lord. And like every other ministry, serving as a pastor of a church replant can be very discouraging at times. It can be discouraging when young families come and visit, but don't stay because you can't offer the same types of children's programming that the large church down the street does. It is discouraging when it seems like the congregation is not catching your vision for living on mission and reaching the lost in the community. It can be discouraging when it feels like even the smallest change you try to implement is met with pushback for all kinds of silly reasons. This is why it is so vital that partner churches intentionally work to encourage, assist, and cooperate with the replanter and his family over the long haul.

REASON 2: REPLANTING CAN BE LONELY.

Many pastors are incredibly lonely in ministry. Loneliness is one of the leading factors for why a large number of pastors quit ministry altogether. This is especially true in smaller congregations in more rural areas. Many replants will take place in these types of communities. Regardless of where the replant is located, partner churches must recognize the loneliness many replanters and their families experience. A partner church must help them fight against this feeling of loneliness that is so common in ministry.

REASON 3: REPLANTING IS HARD WORK.

Replanting a congregation is really hard work. No pastor can do this on his own. He needs help and resources from other churches and individuals. Whether through financial support, words of love and encouragement, the sending of teams to work on the building, sharing program ideas and ministry supplies or whatever else it looks like, a partner church can take ownership of helping the replant in as many ways as possible. A partner church can help lighten the load so that this replanting work is a joy (and not a burden) for the replanter and his family. Radical, eager, selfless cooperation is needed. What exactly should long-haul encouragement, cooperation, and assistance look like practically?

THE REPLANT CARE TEAM

Replanters often struggle in the ministry of church revitalization because they can feel alone. They feel discouraged and are not surrounded by many, if any, encouragers. They are dealing with criticism from members, and face the challenge of reaching new families. They have to learn a new church culture, and have likely left all of their friends. They are working long hours for little pay. Add to this we are all fighting against an enemy that seeks to kill and destroy the work of God. Replanting is a battle and partner churches can intentionally join them on the front lines through assembling a replanter care team.

What is a Replanter Care Team?

The replanter care team is a group of individuals, appointed by the *Replant Partner Team (see Chapter 2)* that work together for the purpose of caring for and encouraging the replanter and his family. At a minimum, the replanter care team should be comprised of a pastor from the partner church along with at least two others who have a special interest and care for the replanter and his family. These people should have the gift of encouragement, time, a heart for God and a passion for replanting. One of the church members should be designated as the team leader and point person.

The team should meet once a month for about an hour. In addition to this monthly meeting, the team should also plan to meet for one extended meeting once a year, probably during the month of January, to discuss long term goals for the year. During the monthly meeting the team will pray, plan and implement care for the replanter.

Pray: Pray specifically for the replanter and his family.

Plan: Planning may consist of a long-term calendar and short-term goals for supporting and encouraging the replanter and his family. A Care Plan should be developed by the team clearly laying out specific ways in which the partner church will show love and care to the replanter and his family on a month-to-month basis over the course of a year. The monthly team meeting will serve as a regular touch point to strategize for what is next in the Care Plan and ensure that someone on the team is taking the lead on particular items of support.

Implement: Each meeting should assign responsibilities to team members and other partner church members who can be involved in the Care Plan. Remember, the purpose of this team is not to do all the work of caring and encouraging, but to mobilize the partner church to also help. This is a wonderful way to assist the partner church members, helping them to stay closely connected to the replanter and his family.

You will know you've had a successful meeting when team members leave with action items that will encourage and support the replanter and his family in the days ahead.

How Will the Team Know it's Been Successful?

There are two very simple components to success: 1) Ensuring the team continues to implement the Care Plan and 2) regular communication (at least every 3 months) to receive honest feedback directly from the replanter about the success of the care plan. (If you find the care plan is not meeting the needs of the replanter and his family, adjust the plan as needed.)

Let's now consider some specific ways the care team can intentionally work with and help mobilize the partner church to care for the replanter and his family in an intentional and consistent manner. First, here are some helpful ways to partner with the replanter.

COMING ALONGSIDE THE REPLANTER

Sermon Help

Many times, it can be helpful for the replanting pastor to work with the pastor of a partner church in doing a sermon series together. This can be a great way for mentoring to happen, especially if the replanting pastor is younger in ministry. It is a blessing for the replanter to benefit from the coaching of a more experienced pastor, and it is a blessing for the partner church pastor to encourage the replanter however he can. Teamwork is crucial in replanting. This is also true when it comes to growing as preachers and teachers of the Word—the more cooperation and teamwork, the better it is for both congregations.

Sharing Books

Most pastors love books. In most replants, there is very little budget for pastors to purchase new books and resources for ongoing growth and development. The partner church can help with this by buying or sharing books with the replanter. You may want to create a budget line item specifically for the development and growth of the replanter, just as you would any other staff member from the partner congregation. This will be a huge blessing to the pastor and will encourage him and his growth as a leader.

Conferences

Whenever possible, invite (and pay) for the replanting pastor to go to conferences with the staff of the partner church. Conferences are so helpful in caring for the soul of leaders. Many pastors in smalller churches are unable to afford to go to conferences of any kind. Help the replanter get to a conference, and even further help him by finding someone to fill the pulpit for the weekend after the conference. What a blessing this will be!

Monthly Video Call

It is helpful to schedule a monthly video call with the replanter.[10] A video call is preferred over a regular phone call because you are able to look at the replanter and engage with him in a more personal and intimate manner than a simple phone call. I would recommend having the lead pastor and one or two other leaders from the partner church be part of this call. Having this monthly time set up as a consistent touchpoint allows the replanter a safe place to share needs and concerns, get ideas on how to deal with difficult situations, and simply be encouraged. This kind of safe outlet for ongoing care and coaching is something a partner church can supply very easily.

A Regularly Scheduled Face-to-Face Meeting

Depending on distance, it is important to regularly schedule a face-to-face meeting with key leaders from the partner church and the replanter. It might be helpful for a few other core leaders from the replant to join in this meeting as well. There is nothing like spending time together in person, laughing together, talking together, dreaming together, praying together. This is also a chance to hear updates on what God is doing in the replant, as well as discuss any current challenges they are dealing with. And of course, this meeting should take place over food (good food). And the partner church should buy!

Calls and Texts of Encouragement

Never underestimate the power of a quick, encouraging phone call or text message. Make it a habit to regularly let the replanter know the partner church is thankful for him and are praying for him. Any chance you get to affirm and build a replanter up in some way, do it. It will mean the world to him and will be a joy for you.

COMING ALONGSIDE THE REPLANTER'S WIFE AND CHILDREN

While it is critical for the partner church to intentionally work to encourage and care for the replanter, it is just as important that they care for and support the replanter's wife and children. Ministry of any kind can be very hard on a pastor's family. Replanting a church brings unique pressures and challenges that not only affect the replanter, but affect his wife and kids as well. A partner church must prioritize showing extra love and encouragement to the replanter's family. Here are some ideas to implement.

Monthly Video Call with the Replanter's Wife

One of the great ways you can serve the replanter's wife is through ongoing, intentional encouragement through a monthly video call with other pastor's or leader's wives from the partner church. This is an opportunity to hear about challenges and struggles she may be having. It also gives her a regular outlet to laugh and pray with other godly women outside of the replant. It is an opportunity to befriend her and love her with the love of Jesus. Having a couple women from the partner church own this and schedule the meeting calls is highly recommended.

Sending Gift Cards and Flowers

Another way to regularly encourage a replanter's wife and kids is to surprise them with special gifts periodically. Gift cards to a favorite local restaurant, toy store, book store, gift store, or spa (for *mom,* of course) might be exactly what they need. Sending a bouquet of flowers from time to time is a simple, thoughtful gesture to express your care for the replanter's wife. Be intentional about surprising them with these types of thoughtful gifts.

Special Visits

Be intentional about scheduling the replanter and his family for a yearly visit to the partner church. When they come, treat them like royalty—get them a nice hotel if they are coming from out of town. Take care of all of their meals. Set the replanting pastor and his wife up with a special date night and provide childcare. Get creative and try to make these trips full of fun surprises for the replanting family.

Notes of Encouragement

Another way you can get the partner congregation involved in caring for the replanter's wife and children is by having them regularly send special notes of encouragement. Few things are more uplifting than a kind word from a friend. This is a great ministry that can involve all different ages of folks from the partner church. For example, elderly members who are not able to be part of other ministries in the church can help out with the special encouragement ministry. Perhaps your church can get into the rhythm of sending a large bundle of encouragement notes to the replanter's family once every few months, or spread them out and send a few notes each week. Whatever you decide to do, this is a great way to care for this dear family.

Books and Magazines

Select a "book of the month" or subscribe to magazines and devotional guides to send to the replanter's wife and children. This will be an ongoing source of encouragement and edification for them. Moreover, it shows the wife and children that the partner church cares for the spiritual health of everyone in the family, and not just the replanting pastor. This communicates a lot to the family and also to the members of the replant.

Invite the Replanter's Wife to Women's Events

Even if she is unable to come to many of the women's events happening at the partner church, it would be great if you can find a way for her to take part in some of the major events throughout the year. Sometimes, this means finding trusted and reliable childcare for her kids. Chances are that in the replant, there will be very few opportunities for her to focus on her own spiritual growth and fellowship with other godly women. The partner church can help immensely with this. Giving a replanter's wife an opportunity to attend a conference or special event can be a great encouragement to her.

Birthday Cards

Sending personal cards to the replanter's wife and children on their birthdays is a wonderful reminder to them that the partner congregation cares about them and is thinking about them. Be sure to send a fun little gift on their birthday as well!

A few ideas...

To encourage the whole family:

- Zoo Day
- Professional Baseball Game
- Weekend in the mountains or at the beach
- Amusement park/water park Day
- Surprise cookie tray/popcorn/cupcakes sent to the family
- Family movie night at home package – (Redbox, pizza, popcorn)

To encourage the replanter's wife:

- Bundle of encouraging notes and texts
- Starbucks gift card and a book
- Gift certificate to have the house cleaned
- Spa gift card
- Surprise lunch with other pastor's/leader's wives

IT'S ALL ABOUT THE LONG HAUL...

Coming alongside and serving a replanter and his family should not be a burden, but privilege and joy for a partner church! The replant needs this kind of ongoing support and steady encouragement. The replanter's wife and kids need faithful love and support, not just for a few days or weeks, but months and even years into the future. May we see many congregations than willingly choose to love these dear families with the intentional, radical, selfless, love of Jesus over the long haul.

PATHWAY TO PARTNERSHIP

Partnership allows everyone to pitch in!

It has been a joy for our family to partner with Summitview, a new replant in our community. Let me share a few reasons why you may want to consider intentional partnership with a new replant as well.

First, partnering with a replant will refocus you on the mission. There are just too many lost people in our city and not enough gospel churches. According to the information on City-Data's website, there are thirty-two thousand people in the zip code for the replant we are part of. And 66% of the population in in our community does not claim any religion, whereas evangelicals are merely 11%. Partnering with a replant reminds you that the gospel is advancing, but there's much work left to do.

Next, partnering with a replant will get you involved more deeply in local church life. Since a replant is smaller, everyone can pitch in and help in different areas, from greeting, nursery, music, and hospitality. You can't come in, smile, make small talk, and then sit back and enjoy the music and preaching only to leave several hours later. Because replants are smaller, they're more personal, which means you're never serving alone. Partnering with a replant is a great way to discover your gifts, as you make new friends.

– *Adam Embry,* Member of a new Replant

PART THREE
DISCUSSION QUESTIONS

Creating Thriving Partnerships

1. What are some of the main reasons why partnerships struggle? What do you believe are some of the causes for these partnership struggles?

2. As you consider the five pillars of effective partnership, which of these will be easiest for your congregation? Why? Which will be most difficult? Why?

3. Have you and your potential partner determined how the following will be handled as you form a partnership together?

   Expectations and Roles:

   - Facilities:
   - Membership:
   - Holidays and special services:
   - Worship Style:
   - Existing/New Ministries:
   - Theological distinctions:
   - Finances:
   - Baggage/Culture:

PART 4

A ROADMAP FOR PARTNERSHIP

Chapter 12

MAKING IT OFFICIAL:
Writing a Partnership Agreement

There aren't many things as beautiful as witnessing a marriage ceremony between two godly people.

Two different histories.

Two different family backgrounds.

Two different worlds coming together as one.

It is absolutely beautiful and the Lord is honored in this. One man and one woman united together in Jesus Christ giving their lives to one another before God, their families and friends. One man and one woman committing to love one another through thick and thin, good and bad, sickness and health, riches and poverty. The marriage ceremony where these commitments are made symbolize the official beginning of their new life together.

While there may not be a "marriage ceremony" that marks the official beginning of a church partnership, it is important to take seriously the commitment involved as two congregations move forward with one another in unity. A clear and agreed-upon commitment is critical for the partnership to be all that God wants it to be. For this reason, we want to consider some of the steps involved in developing an official partnership agreement.

The following six steps can help guide the designated leaders from each church as they seek to develop a plan for how best to move into the future together as partners. These steps are designed to help provide structure and direction for the actual typing up of an agreement. Our hope is that this will make this important component of the partnership process as clear, smooth, enjoyable and effective as possible for everyone involved. What designated leaders should be part of this process? We recommend having the following individuals involved:

-   **From the replant:** The replanting pastor and a few other key leaders.

-   **From the partner church:** A pastor and a few members of the partner team.

This group of individuals will be charged with creating the agreed upon partner agreement that will be used by both churches moving forward.

STEP 1: DEFINE THE LEVEL, TYPE AND PURPOSE OF THIS PARTNERSHIP.

The first step in the process of writing a partnership agreement is to be crystal-clear on the level, type and purpose of this partnership. Look back at Chapters 6 and 7 where we discuss the different levels and types of partnership. The *Partnership Pyramid* that we introduced in Chapter 7 can serve as a tool to help both congregations assess, discern and discuss which type of partnership would be best to pursue. It may be helpful to print out copies of the *Partnership Pyramid* to give to everyone involved in the writing of this agreement.

STEP 2: ARTICULATE THE GOALS OF THE PARTNERSHIP.

After determining the level and type of partnership the churches will pursue, it's important to articulate the goals of this partnership. In other words, *"What are you aiming for?"* I've heard it said, "If you aim at nothing, you'll hit it every time!" This is particularly true when it comes to effective church partnership. Taking the time needed to articulate clear goals will help immensely in making sure you accomplish exactly what is desired. How many goals you choose to set is up to you—just make sure they are the right kinds of goals.

Naturally, the next question is: What kinds of goals should you set? Let us encourage you to spend time developing what is often referred to as, S.M.A.R.T. goals. While there are different variations of S.M.A.R.T. goals, we would say they are goals, which are marked by five things. They are:

1. Specific.
2. Measurable.
3. Achievable.
4. Relevant.
5. Timely.

Consider each of these components that will help you set effective partnership goals:[11]

Set SPECIFIC Goals

When setting goals for church partnership, you need to be specific about what you hope to accomplish. Your goals must be clear and well defined. Vague or generalized goals are not helpful, because they don't provide sufficient direction. Remember—you need goals to show you the way. Make it as easy as you can to get where you want to go by defining precisely *where* you want to end up.[12]

Set MEASURABLE Goals

How will you know when you have met your goal? This moves your goal from being abstract to more concrete. Set milestones along the way so that you are not caught off guard and so that you can track your progress.

Set ACHIEVABLE Goals

Your goals should inspire you, not discourage you. If you set a goal you can't possibly reach, you'll continually feel defeated. It can take a bit of time to refine this step, but it is still important.

Take note of the skills, people, finances and tools you will need to have in place to achieve the goal.

Set RELEVANT Goals

If your goal doesn't truly benefit the mission of helping the replant become healthy, growing and on mission, why do it? Every goal should move both churches in the direction of the larger mission: To make joyful, passionate disciples of Jesus Christ for the glory of God.

Set TIMELY Goals

Make sure you give yourself enough time to achieve your goals, but also to be intentional with the time. Your goals must always have a clear deadline. It means that you know when you can celebrate success. When you are working on a deadline, your sense of urgency increases and achievement will come that much quicker. After you figure out the final deadline, set checkpoints where you can make sure you are still on target time-wise.

STEP 3: LAY OUT THE SPECIFIC RESPONSIBILITIES FOR EACH CHURCH.

Some of the responsibilities may come to light as you are creating your S.M.A.R.T. goals together. However, we recommend taking the time in this third step to make sure everyone is clear on what the specific responsibilities are for each church moving forward.

The worst thing you can do is assume in a partnership. To assume the other church is going to do this or that, or give this or that, or lead this or that. Never assume anything. *Go the extra mile to be clear on what the particular responsibilities are for each congregation and together agree on them.* You may want to review Chapter 7, which helps to explain what some of these responsibilities might be depending on the level and type of partnership being pursued.

STEP 4: AGREE ON WHAT RESOURCES AND FINANCES WILL BE COMMITTED.

One indisputable principle in the life of every church is this: ministry requires resources. Whether it's human capital, intellectual energy, artistic creativity or money, every form of ministry requires kingdom-oriented capital.

As two churches explore partnering together the resource conversation, is not only necessary, it is *important.* Differing levels of partnership require differing levels of commitment and conversation. If you review the *Partnership Pyramid,* it is readily apparent as you climb toward the top, a greater commitment is made in resourcing.

- Sending Church Partnership: High level of resource investment
- Strategic Church Partnership: Mid level of resource investment
- Supporting Church Partnership: Low level of resource investment

Here are some of the considerations and conversations that will be necessary have as two churches explore joining together for the sake of kingdom impact.

Legal and Financial Consultation

Every state and municipality differs in what it requires of nonprofits and organizational entities in terms of reporting, legal documents and accounting. It is important that partnerships where two churches will be joining resources, assuming ownership of property, and potentially dissolving one church into the receivership of another receives legal and financial counsel. We recommend checking with your state convention or local denominational association to assist in this. Organizations like the Church Law Group of Texas may be able to provide advice on all these matters.

Create an Assets and Debt List

Scripture offers some wise advice: "Be sure you know the condition of your flocks, give careful attention to your herds."[13] In sending partnerships in particular, it will be important to obtain a full account of assets and debts of both organizations, understanding the terms of loans and amounts in reserves or investments. Getting the financial officers and committees of both churches together is one good first step toward getting this information flowing. We recommend obtaining actual bank statements as well as accounting reports form the church files.

Pre-Existing Contracts and Obligations

In some cases, churches enter into lease or rental agreements for equipment or facility with other churches or organizations. More often than not, these are written agreements, but in some cases you may discover "handshake" agreements made by people with good intentions. Practice due diligence in accounting for all obligations and contracts, written or not.

Financial Reserves and Designated Funds

Struggling churches may have significant sums tied up in designated funds or investments which were meant to be a blessing but may have become a burden. It's possible that funds are not readily available for ministry or have been earmarked for a purpose that is no longer feasible or possible. There is a difference between what is legally permissible and culturally permissible in dealing with such funds. We recommend consulting with an accountant familiar with funds and church finances to determine how to handle these funds going forward.

Establish a Budget

Moving forward, both churches will be contributing to the ministry needs of the new church. Both bodies will bring people and resources to the table, and both should contribute proportionately according to need and ability. Here are some general guidelines as you sit down to form one new budget for the partnership.

- Base the budget on current levels of giving from the giving records[14] of those who have committed to the new partnership.

- Include amounts committed from the stronger partnering church. (In some cases support or start-up funds are given, and should be included in a yearly ministry budget, not simply saved for "rainy" day reserve funds.)

- Anticipate economic decline. As a general rule, churches can expect to see a 20% decline in giving from legacy members as changes begin to occur. Monitor closely and adjust as necessary.

- Plan for building remodel, repair and upgrades. A struggling and declining church typically has deferred maintenance and modernization of facilities and decor. Significant investments may need to be made in the start up of the new partnership.

Property Ownership

In some cases, it may be wise and prudent for the original congregation to maintain legal ownership of the property and building. When property changes owners, it can trigger facility inspections that require all features of the facility to meet current building codes. This could prove untenable, in that the upgrades may become cost-prohibitive and derail the partnership. Consider filing a *DBA* (Doing Business As) designation with the Secretary of State to avoid potential costly facility upgrades when property changes ownership.

STEP 5: MAKE A COMMITMENT TO COMMUNICATE.

Leaders involved with a church replant need constant encouragement, and lots of it. There are many ups and downs throughout the journey of leading a church from near death back to health and vibrancy. This is why a commitment to communicate is so important. We recommend committing to three types of communication: Monthly updates, quarterly calls, and annual visits.

Monthly Updates

Monthly updates from the replant through letter, email, or video allows the partner congregation to stay up to speed with what the Lord is doing in and through the replant. It also allows the partner congregation to know how best they can pray for and support the replant.

Quarterly Calls

Quarterly phone or video calls between the leaders of the partner and the replant allows for more in-depth conversation between the churches on a somewhat regular basis. These calls are a great opportunity to hear about what God is doing and some of the victories they're experiencing in the replant. It is also a chance to help bring wisdom and counsel to any difficult situations the replant may be experiencing. This quarterly call is huge in helping the leaders of this new replant feel loved, cared for, and equipped for the ministry God has called them to.

Annual Visits

While perhaps the replant and the partner church are located in the same city or community, it is very possible this isn't the case. It may be that the replant and partner church are in different states, on opposite sides of the country, or even the world! If this is the case, it is important to try and schedule annual visits if you are able. We recommend the pastor, his family, and some other leaders from the replant to spend a weekend with the partner church at least once a year. This can be a weekend designed to hear what God is doing through the replant, to celebrate the partnership between the churches and to cast fresh vision for what the partnership will look like for the upcoming year. These weekends can help folks who are new to the partner church catch the excitement that comes with partnering with a replant.

Along with the replant leaders visiting the partner church, it is ideal if the partner church can schedule at least one trip a year to help serve the replant in some way. It may be a youth trip, a family trip, or an intergenerational trip. Whatever it might be, it is an effective way to build deeper friendship with those in the replant while also serving them with the love of Christ. Volunteers can lead VBS, complete work projects in and around the church building, or do some other form of service. An annual trip can be one of the most powerful ways to care for and strengthen the partnership relationship.

STEP 6: PLAN FOR AN ANNUAL EVALUATION OF THE PARTNERSHIP.

The sixth and final step to developing a partnership Agreement is planning for an annual evaluation. Though it is a step often overlooked or skipped, honest evaluation and feedback is vital to the long-term health of any church partnership. Evaluation helps leaders celebrate areas of success, while also identifying areas of needed growth. Along with setting a specific date for the annual review, the following is a list of ten areas to be evaluated on an annual basis. Feel free to add additional questions under each category as needed.

9 Areas of Partnership Evaluation[15]

1. **General**

   - What are we grateful for in this partnership?
   - What have we given and received from one another?
   - Where is the Lord clearly at work in and through this partnership?
   - What do we see as next steps to this partnership?

2. **Partnership Agreement**

   - How have we lived out the partnership agreement?
   - What has been positive? Negative?
   - Does the partnership agreement need to be modified in any way?

3. **Relationships**

   - Are there any tensions or misunderstandings between leaders or churches?
   - Are we communicating well with one another? How can we improve our communication?
   - Is there a strong sense of trust with one another? How can we build more trust?

4. **Goals**

   - What goals have we accomplished?
   - What goals are not accomplished?
   - What new goals or modifications should we make?

5. **Leadership**

- Who are the leaders of this partnership? In what areas has leadership been strong? Weak?
- Is anyone experiencing burnout?
- Is there "new-blood" on your partnership team? Should there be?

6. **Opportunities**

- Are the opportunities for involvement in both directions?
- Are we praying for one another regularly?

7. **Communication**

- How are you sharing news and enthusiasm with both congregations?
- How would you grade the quality of communication at this point? Why?
- How can communication be improved?

8. **Finances**

- Share and review financial and/or resource commitments for both partners.
- Are there any financial questions that need to be addressed?

9. **Renew or Conclude?**

- Do both churches desire to renew their partnership for another year?

- If it is time for the partnership to conclude, how can you make sure the partnership is concluded well for both congregations?
- How might you celebrate what the Lord has done in and through this partnership?

In review, these six steps are designed to help the partnering churches work together to create a clear, practical and effective partnership agreement:

1. Define what level, type and purpose of partnership this will be.
2. Articulate the goals of this partnership.
3. Lay out the specific responsibilities for each church.
4. Agree on what resources and finances will be committed.
5. Make a commitment to communicate: Monthly updates, quarterly calls, and annual visits.
6. Plan for an annual evaluation of the partnership.

In our experience, when the leaders of the partnering churches work through each of these steps in a thorough and unified manner, it helps set the partnership up for great success moving forward. Where there are questions or confusion, seek to go the extra mile to communicate with one another clearly. *Remember, clarity is key.* And clarity takes intentional, over the top conversation and communication.

You can do this. Enjoy the process together!

A Sample Replant Partnership Agreement

When you put all the pieces together, here is just one example of how a Partner Agreement might look. Again, yours will look different as it will include goals and partner strategies that are unique to your partnership.

Partner Church: First Baptist Church

Replant: City View Church

Step #1: The Level, Type, and Purpose of Partnership *(see Partnership Pyramid)*

Partnership Level: Strategic

Partnership Type: Equipping

Partnership Purpose: FBC children's ministry leaders will help equip and encourage the children's ministry leaders of City View as they launch a new ministry to children and their parents. This is an intentional, 1 year partnership that will begin January 1st, 2018 and will conclude December 31st, 2018.

Step #2: The S.M.A.R.T. Goals for this Partnership

1. The FBC children's ministry leadership team will equip the children's ministry leaders of City View through four, three-hour training events over the course of the next calendar year for the purpose of helping them effectively launch and lead their ministry to children and parents.

2. The four trainings will take place on a quarterly basis over the course of the year: One training in Winter, one in Spring, one in Summer, and one in Fall.

3. The focus of each of the trainings will be:
- **Winter:** Biblical and theological foundations for building a God-honoring children's ministry.
- **Spring:** Developing and leading an effective children's ministry volunteer leadership team.
- **Summer:** How to effectively and biblically teach and program for children's ministry (Sunday school, camps and retreats, special events, weeknight programming, etc.)
- **Fall:** Connecting ministry to children in the church with ministry to children in the home (Equipping parents to disciple their kids).

4. The FBC children's ministry leadership team will schedule and lead monthly coaching video calls for the children's ministry leaders of City View. The purpose of these calls will be to bring further instruction, encouragement, and trouble-shooting to the leaders of City View as they are developing their children's ministry over the course of the year. These calls will last anywhere from 1-2 hours depending on the particular needs and issues needed to be addressed.

5. The FBC children's ministry leadership team and the children's ministry leaders of City View will gather for a two day, extended training retreat on June 14-15, 2018. This retreat will take place at John and Susan Hanson's cabin. The purpose of this retreat is to provide an extended time for fellowship, conversation, equipping, and prayer together as children's ministry leaders from both churches. The retreat will be planned and led by The FBC children's ministry leadership team.

Step #3: The Specific Responsibilities for Each Church

Specific responsibilities for FBC:

1. Planning, scheduling, and leading:

- The quarterly training events.
- Monthly video calls.
- Summer training retreat at the Hanson's cabin.

2. Being available for phone call and email interaction to answer questions or trouble shoot with the leaders of City View over the course of the year partnership.

Specific responsibilities for City View:

3. A commitment to be actively engaged in, and committed to:

- The quarterly training events.
- Monthly video calls.
- Summer training retreat at the Hanson's cabin.

4. Hosting the four quarterly training events at City View's building. While the leaders of FBC will be in charge of planning and buying the food for these training events, the leaders of City View will provide a hospitable environment for these events.

5. Providing a monthly, 1-2 page report updating the children's ministry leaders of FBC on:

-   Joys and successes in the children's ministry.
-   Areas of current struggle and challenge.
-   Specific areas of needed help and equipping.
-   Particular prayer requests for the children's ministry and those involved.

Step #4: Resources and Finances that Will Be Committed

FBC will cover all of the expenses and financial needs for this partnership. These will include:

1. All books and other teaching materials needed for the four quarterly trainings.

2. Any and all expenses associated with getting the monthly call set-up for both churches.

3. All food and snacks for the four quarterly trainings.

4. Any additional, unforeseen expenses that arise, which will aid to the health and effectiveness of the partnership.

Step #5: A commitment to communicate

The FBC children's ministry leaders will make the following communication commitments:

1. *Monthly Video Calls* - As mentioned above, the FBC children's ministry leadership team will schedule and lead monthly coaching video calls for the children's ministry leaders of City View. The purpose of these calls will be to bring further instruction, encouragement, and trouble-shooting to the leaders of City View as they are developing their children's ministry over the course of the year. These calls will last anywhere from 1-2 hours depending on the particular needs and issues needed to be addressed.

2. *Phone Calls and Emails* - It is understood that throughout the partnership there will be regular, ongoing communication through phone and email. This will allow for more immediate communication between leaders from each church as questions, issues, and needs arise.

The children's ministry leaders of City View will make the following communication commitments:

1. *Monthly Video Calls* - As mentioned above, the FBC children's ministry leadership team will schedule and lead monthly coaching video calls for the children's ministry leaders of City View. This is an opportunity for monthly connection and communication.

2. *Monthly Updates* - 1-2 page report updating the children's ministry leaders of FBC on:

- Joys and successes in the children's ministry.

- Areas of current struggle and challenge.
- Specific areas of needed help and equipping.
- Particular prayer requests for the children's ministry and those involved.

3. *Phone Calls and Emails* - It is understood that throughout the partnership there will be regular, ongoing communication through phone and email. This will allow for more immediate communication between leaders from each church as questions, issues, and needs arise.

Step #6: Annual evaluation of the partnership

Date: December 18th, 2018

On December 18th, 2018, the children's ministry team leaders from both FBC and City View will gather together for an annual review and evaluation of the partnership. This evaluation meeting will last 2-3 hours. Prior to this meeting, it is expected that the leaders from each church will spend time answering the following evaluation questions. Each leader will then bring their responses to these questions to the meeting, which will help guide the evaluation conversation:

Chapter 13

LAUNCHING THE PARTNERSHIP:
The Four Key Meetings

Now we are going to get super practical. How do we get this partnership process started? There are several meetings that must take place between the leaders of both the partner church and the replant in order to launch well. While there will be numerous phone calls and email interactions throughout this process to discuss questions each church has, email and phone interaction should not take the place of these meetings if at all possible. These meetings should include all of the key leaders from both churches who are leading the way in this partnership initiative.

There may be scenarios in which fewer meetings are needed or where some meetings may be combined. It also might be that you may need to add more meetings. Remember what is most important in all of this—*building trust*. Building trust is absolutely crucial, and it is built through time spent together and through clear, thoughtful communication. The more opportunity for clear communication and time to ask questions, the better. This is why we recommend that all of these meetings take place in person. It may be that a few of these meetings must take place over video call simply due to distance.

In our experience, there is a much better chance for a smooth launch into partnership between the two churches when the meetings take place and are both attended and led well. Let's consider what each of these meetings involve.

MEETING 1: INTRODUCTIONS - GETTING TO KNOW ONE ANOTHER

The first meeting in the partnership process is a simple introductory meeting. This meeting is important because it will help determine whether there is chemistry between the two churches that could potentially lead to a partnership. There are four main topics of discussion that you want to cover in this initial meeting.

> **Goal:** *To get the key leaders from both the partner church and the replant together for the purpose of hearing about the current situation of the replant; the heart of the partner church to help; any areas of disagreement or misalignment; and if there is potential to meet again.*

Topic #1: The Current Situation of the Replant

In this meeting, you will get a general overview of the replant, including their history, affiliations and whether or not there is potential for partnership. You will want to ask a lot of questions and listen to the key leaders of this church as they talk about their congregation. What are some of the challenges they are experiencing currently? What is the current makeup of the congregation? What types of needs do they currently have? You want to get as much information as you can about this church.

Topic #2: The Heart of the Partner Church to Help Replanted Congregations

Along with learning as much as you can about the history and current status of the replant, this meeting is an important opportunity to share the heart behind the partner church's desire to come alongside and help the church experience new life and vibrancy. This is the time to communicate your passion to see God revitalize dying churches for his glory. If your own church has experienced revitalization on some level, this is a great opportunity to share what God has done in and through your congregation.

I know for our church, there is no greater joy for our people than to share how we were once a dying church and realizing that God was not done with us. By his grace, he breathed new life into our congregation for the sake of the lost, the good of our community and ultimately, for his glory. Sharing what God has done in your church can inspire and bring hope to these leaders, reminding them that God desires to do something special through them. Cast the vision of how God has now given your church a desire to come alongside replants like theirs to serve them and encourage them.

A Replant Partner Team

What is it and how do we put one together? Strong, committed leadership is critical to any healthy church partnership. And as discussed in Chapter 3, we recommend putting together a *Replant Partner Team* that can help mobilize and lead a partner church in the partnership process. While a pastor should be part of this team, it is important that other individuals from the congregation are actively involved as well. This team should be made up of a diverse group of men and women (and sometimes youth).

Our hope is that the *Replant Partner Team* try to meet every 4-6 weeks over the course of a year. These meetings should be anywhere from one to two hours in length. This regularly scheduled meeting together will allow the team to strategize and determine ways to consistently mobilize the congregation to be involved in the partnership. Remember: It is not the job of this team to carry the entire load of the partnership, but rather, this team helps to cast vision and plug in the members of the congregation to use their gifts and get involved in the partnership in some way.

Are there any areas of significant disagreement or misalignment?

As is appropriate, you want to begin to discern whether there are any areas of significant disagreement or misalignment with a potential partner church. Outlined below are six key areas of alignment that churches should aim for. These include theology, secondary matters, finances, denomination/networks, leadership, and vision/strategy. The level of alignment in these six areas will help to determine whether or not partnership is a possibility or not. If partnership is a possibility, where each congregation stands in regard to these areas will help determine the types of partnership that might be pursued. While you might not be able to discuss all of these areas in the first meeting together, you should try to address some of them.

Take some time to compile the answers to these questions, so that through prayer, discernment and discussion you can determine how best to move forward with the other church.

When Evaluating a Potential Partner Church:

6 Questions for 6 Key Areas

1. **Theology.** Where is there alignment in theology? Where is there not?

2. **Secondary Matters.** What secondary values, convictions and traditions are shared between your congregations? Which ones are not? Are these significant enough to hinder an effective partnership?

3. **Finances.** What financial roadblocks might stand in the way of your partnership?

4. **Denomination/Networks.** Are there any denominational or network conflicts that could hinder your partnership? What expectations come with the resources they might offer?

5. **Leadership.** Who are the leaders of this church? Do you feel you can trust their leaders? How have they demonstrated their trustworthiness? Do you have any initial concerns with their motives or readiness?

6. **Vision/Strategy.** How well do you align with the other church's vision and strategy? Is there enough alignment in ministry philosophy that you can partner together, or are there significant differences that could make healthy partnership a challenge?

Is there potential enough to meet again for further conversation?

Once you have spent time learning about one another's congregations, discussing the current state of the replant and the vision of the partner church to come alongside and help replants through partnership, it will become pretty clear whether the conversation needs to continue into a second meeting. If so, the second meeting will focus on what the process of partnership will look like.

MEETING 2 - DEFINING THE RELATIONSHIP

Building off information gathered from the first meeting and additional communication between church leaders, the second meeting is focused on defining the relationship between the congregations. What exactly will this partnership look like, what will be involved, and what steps will be needed to move forward?

> **Goal:** *To clearly define the relationship between the two churches moving forward. By the end of this meeting, it must be clear to the leaders of both congregations what exactly the*

partnership is and what would need to happen to officially enter into a partnership relationship.

In this meeting, go over the different levels and types of potential partnership discussed earlier in the book. It would be wise to print out copies of the Partnership Pyramid for those at this meeting, helping to make sure that everyone understands the type of partnership that is being proposed.

Over-communicate everything in this meeting. Be crystal clear on what it will mean and what it will not mean to be involved with each type of partnership. Fuzziness will come back to bite you later on. As you go over the specifics of partnership and what it means for the two congregations to move in that direction, you can anticipate many questions from leaders. This is a good thing—clarity is critical to healthy partnership. Take your time in this meeting to give all leaders involved an accurate picture of what is coming if the churches choose to move forward in partnership. This meeting should conclude with both churches committing to fervently pray about the potential partnership before the next meeting.

MEETING 3 - DETERMINING THE DIRECTION

In the third meeting, it should be fairly clear whether or not the leaders of each of the churches desire to pursue partnership (and what type of partnership). Much conversation and interaction will have taken place, and many questions and concerns will have been addressed. This meeting allows for further clarification to be given and remaining questions and concerns to be addressed.

Goal: *Determine which direction the two churches desire to go. Do they want to pursue partnership, or is it best to lovingly part ways? If partnership is the desired direction, a partnership agreement laying out the specific type of partnership and commitments involved will be discussed and developed together.*

Typically, by the time of this meeting, a church that has no interest in pursuing a partnership has let the leaders of the other congregation know. In cases where the partnership conversation has ended, a third meeting never actually takes place. But there are times when this third meeting provides the clarity needed for one or both of the congregations to back out of any potential partnership. While this decision might be disappointing, it is much better to lovingly part ways at this point than to keep walking down a road that has no real future.

Typically, it is during this meeting that leaders of both churches work together to discuss and develop a partnership agreement to be voted on by each congregation. Because of the time it will take to develop the agreement, this may be the longest of the meetings.

Special Note

We realize that depending on the level and type of partnership being pursued, you may not be able to create and finish an agreement in one meeting together. You may need several additional interactions and discussions to create the agreement—that is fine. Do what is most helpful and effective for your partnership. Clarity and unity moving forward is the key. Take the time that you need to achieve this.

The previous chapter explains in detail the steps involved in developing a partnership agreement. You may want to print out a copy of the main steps involved in developing a partnership agreement to give to those present at the meeting to help guide the time together as a group. This is an exciting place to be! It is exhilarating seeing leaders from both churches dreaming about what God can do in and through this partnership.

MEETING 4 - VOTING TO MOVE FORWARD WITH PARTNERSHIP

The fourth meeting will be two separate meetings, but they serve the same purpose: *Both the partner church and the replant vote to move forward with partnership.* It serves as an opportunity for the leaders of each church to cast a compelling vision for church partnership and to share the joy and privilege it is to partner with the other congregation in particular. Tell the story of God's work in the other church, show pictures, and help the members see how exciting it is to partner with this specific congregation.

Goal: *To cast vision to each of the congregations; explaining what partnership is; what it involves; and then to officially vote to move forward together in partnership.*

At this meeting, it is wise to share with members the partnership agreement that has been developed by the leaders of the two congregations. The meeting allows time for members of each congregation to ask questions and share any concerns they might have about moving forward. Ideally, there would be a handful of representatives from each congregation present at each of the meetings. This way leaders are present and available to respond to specific questions that might arise. If they are unable to be there in person, it is recommended to have them be part of the meeting through a video call (so they can be present and interact with those in the meeting as needed).

Upon the churches officially voting to move forward in partnership, it is great to celebrate! Another reason to have representatives from the other congregation in attendance is so you can celebrate together. This is a big deal and leaders should make a big deal of it.

THE JOURNEY OF PARTNERSHIP BEGINS...

As you can see, effective partnership takes intentional, strategic preparation and planning in addition to patience, discernment, love, and much prayer. There are numerous moving pieces and parts in this partnership process, and many individuals are involved within different phases of the journey. But at the end of the day, all of the strategic planning and leading is pointless and powerless apart from the work of the Holy Spirit guiding and saturating each and every component along the way. When a dying church is replanted, it is a supernatural work of God. It is the result of the living, gracious, sovereign Lord of the universe doing what only He can do—bringing dead bones back to life!

Church partnership is one of the primary means God uses in the process of congregational revitalization and renewal. Our prayer is that more and more churches would pursue this kind of intentional replanting partnership. May your congregation help pave the way in this; that the lost might be saved, communities would be transformed, and our great God glorified in the way that he alone deserves.

PATHWAY TO PARTNERSHIP

Partnership brings needed encouragement.

As a lead replanter, I cannot imagine doing this without the support of partner churches. The journey has been tough, but God has continued to empower me to bring gospel-centered life into this dying church through partnerships. Blanca, CO is a rural town of 300 in population, which comes with several difficulties including sometimes feeling very alone. On its own, ministry is hard but even more-so when there is an absence of other leaders to help take the burden of shepherding a hurting flock. However, through my partnerships with other congregations, I am continually reminded that I am not alone as I find others rejoicing with me as I rejoice and mourning with me as I mourn.

Throughout the first couple of months here in Blanca, it looked like everything was quickly falling apart as changes were being implemented. Elders were resigning, and our greatest advocates were turning against us. To make matters even more challenging, previous members from a church split years ago began coming back in mass to our new replant as they heard a new pastor was in town, which poked many wounds in the hearts of current members. My wife and I were beside ourselves as we were accused of asking these previous members to return, which we did not, and even current members of the church were wrapped up in their own conflicts. All we desired to do was to get people to look at Jesus and engage in healthy conflict/resolution in a God-glorifying way.

All this to say, my wife and I would have fallen into despair and wanted to give up if it weren't for other churches, in particular our sending church, continually pouring into us as they pointed us to Jesus on a weekly and sometimes daily basis. I have been meeting weekly with fellow replanters and leaders from other churches through video chats and we have had several teams of people from other congregations come and serve our replant. Jesus continually sustains me through our partnerships. We could not do what we are doing here in Blanca without other Godly men and women pouring into us on a regular basis, keeping my vision and hope in Christ afresh.

– *Mathew Leonard,* Replanting Pastor

PART FOUR
DISCUSSION QUESTIONS

A Roadmap for Partnership

1. How will our congregations spend time developing and deepening our relationship in order to strengthen our partnership?

2. Are we aware which common roadblocks to partnerships might become issues for us in our forming partnership?

3. How will we exercise and display humility in our role as a stronger or weaker/struggling church?

4. Have we drafted a Covenant or Partnership Agreement document?

5. How will we communicate the commitments we are agreeing to for both congregations as they join together?

6. How will we evaluate our commitments regularly to ensure we are being faithful do what and as we promised to one another?

NOTES

[1] Bret Bone, "A Creative Partnership," *Sermoncentral.com*, March 24, 2015, accessed November 15, 2017, https://www.sermoncentral.com/illustrations/sermon-illustration-sermoncentral--stories-intercession-83980?+ref=TextIllustrationSerps.

[2] "The Power of Partnership," *Advance*, accessed November 15, 2017, http://www.advancemovement.com/about/2-the-power-of-partnership/.

[3] Ibid.

[4] For a more extensive and detailed guide on how to replant dying congregations, see Mark Hallock, *Replant Roadmap: How Your Congregation Can Help Revitalize Dying Churches* (Denver, CO: Acoma Press).

[5] "Supporting Church Expectations," *NAMB*, accessed December 1, 2017, https://www.namb.net/Resources/Supporting%20Church%20Expectations.pdf.

[6] Typically, a supporting church does not engage in long term financial commitments to personnel.

[7] "Best Practices of a Sending Church," *NAMB*, accessed December 1, 2017, https://www.namb.net/Resources/Sending%20Church%20Best%20Practices.pdf.

[8] Timothy J. Keller, *The Freedom of Self-Forgetfulness* (Leyland, Lancashire: 10Publishing, 2017), 32.

[9] See 1 Corinthians 16:5-9.

[10] There are many excellent, affordable, easy to use options for video calling. Two recommendations worth considering are *Skype* and *Zoom*.

[11] Adapted from the article "SMART Goals," *Willyouththrive.com*, accessed October 20, 2017, thriverswanted.com/smart.pdf.

[12] Adapted from the article "Golden Rules of Goal Setting," *Mindtools.com*, accessed January 18, 2018, https://www.mindtools.com/pages/article/newHTE_90.htm.

[13] See Proverbs 27:23.

[14] Each church handles access to giving records differently. You are looking for monthly and annual amounts on which you can develop a strong estimate. To build this draft budget secure commitment cards from existing and new members who will be part of the new church and estimate income from historic giving records. Delegating this to a financial team composed of member of both churches is wise and recommended.

[15] Adapted from "A Global Church Partnership Handbook," *Global Ministries*, October 2009, accessed February 15, 2018, http://d3n8a8pro7vhmx.cloudfront.net/globalministries/legacy_url/534/Revised-GCP-Handbook-for-web.pdf?1419962364.

Get the resource which is empowering a movement of church revitalization.

"Mark Hallock is one of the most important voices in this unprecedented need in the modern day to revitalize dying churches. *Replant Roadmap* is sure to become the practical how-to guide to lead this next generation into this noble work."

Brian Croft, Senior Pastor, Auburndale Baptist Church; Senior Fellow, Church Revitalization Center, The Southern Baptist Theological Seminary

the
Replant
Series

This series features short, action-oriented resources
aimed at equipping the North American church for a
movement of church replanting, introduced by Pastor
Mark Hallock's book *Replant Roadmap*.

Thousands of churches are closing their doors in
United States every year in some of its fastest-growing,
most under-reached neighborhoods. Yet there is much
hope for these churches, particularly through the
biblically-rooted, gospel-saturated work of replanting.

Designed for both group and individual study, these
books will help you understand what the Bible has to
say about how God builds and strengthens his church
and offer you some practical steps toward revitalization
in your own.

For more information, visit **acomapress.org** and **nonignorable.org**

ACOMA PRESS

Acoma Press exists to make Jesus non-ignorable by equipping and encouraging churches through gospel-centered resources.

Toward this end, each purchase of an Acoma Press resource serves to catalyze disciple-making and to equip leaders in God's Church. In fact, a portion of your purchase goes directly to funding planting and replanting efforts in North America and beyond. To see more of our current resources, visit us at *acomapress.org*.

Thank you.